A Father's Story

Life
Lessons
from
My Dad
to You

**KAYLYN MARTINEZ
WITH MARK MARTINEZ**

Published by CROP Publishing
Hayden, Idaho
www.AFathersStory.dad
www.MarkMartinez1.com

A Father's Story – Life Lessons from My Dad to You

Copyright @ CROP Publishing 2024

ISBN: 979-8-9900178-0-1

No part of this book may be reproduced in any form by any mechanical means, including information storage and retrieval systems – except in the case of brief quotations embodied in articles or reviews – without permission from the author.

Cover and Interior Design: Beryl Glass

Printed in the United States of America

"All things are possible for the one who believes." – Mark 9:23

Dedication

To all the women and men, girls and boys,

who didn't have the dad they needed in their life.

From Kaylyn

It was 2021 and Father's Day was fast approaching. I wanted to get my dad something. What do you get a man for Father's Day who seems to have everything? In the past, I always purchased stuff that he really enjoyed, but that he often wouldn't purchase on his own. This included beef jerky, beef sticks, and his two favorite guilt-inducing cereals: Trix and Lucky Charms. Simple, yes. But I've learned my dad (like most men) are pretty simple and have very basic needs.

I was in Target, shopping for some normal things, and I happened to pass the book section. I looked around and I found this book titled *Your Father's Story: Dad, I want to know everything about you...* I picked it up and started looking through it. It was a blank journal. Each page had a question at the top pertaining to a dad's story, followed by blank lines below for him to fill out his thoughts, recollections, and advice. It was pretty comprehensive and covered several stages of a father's life. I wasn't positive my dad would fill it out, but if anyone would have done so, it would be my dad. Plus, it was the most original gift I could come across at that time.

When I gave it to him that Father's Day, he was really excited to receive it. He thumbed through the pages and read several of the questions. He said, "I'm going to fill this out. I really am!"

Over the ensuing months, he would give me updates on how he was progressing, but he never shared a single answer that he wrote. Naturally, I was curious to get even a glimpse of what he could have written, but he kept it from me until he was ready to give me back the completed journal.

As he was nearing the end, he shared the idea of publishing the journal as a book, dedicated to all those who didn't have a connected father in their life. On one hand, I was thinking this journal should be a private "love letter" back to me only. Yet, on the other hand, I recalled how many of my friends growing up told me, "I wish I had a dad like yours." I know my dad's heart, and there is enough of it to share with others, so that is why I wanted to share my dad with you. I hope you find something within these pages that can provide you with a similar type of comfort, security, encouragement, and love that I received from my dad.

From Mark

I will always remember the Father's Day that Kaylyn gave me the journal as a gift. I thought, "This is pretty cool. I really love the questions. I'm going to do this!" That evening, I wrote my first entry. The next day, I wrote another one. After a while, I realized that this was a lot of work! This was going to take me longer than I expected. I wanted to put honest thought into each answer. I rarely read ahead, as I wanted to read a question and then answer it based on what first came to mind. I would write an answer or two a day, then I'd have a time gap between my next writings. Weeks turned into months, and I finally completed the journal in just under two years. I returned the journal to Kaylyn as her Mother's Day gift in 2023. Funny thing, though. When she opened her gift and saw that I had completed it, I immediately took it back from her. I didn't want her to read any answers, so that we could capture her real time response to each question live as we recorded each episode for our vlog.

    I would highly encourage you to either offer a journal to your dad or mom, or complete one yourself for your kids. You can either purchase a hard copy, or a downloadable editable PDF. I believe you just might be amazed at what you will receive or have to offer.

www.piccadillyinc.com

https://piccadillyinc.com/products-2/your-stories/

Table of Contents

Acknowledgements (from Kaylyn) 10

Acknowledgements (from Mark) 11

Preface 12

Definitions and Insights (from Mark) 15

Chapter 1 – About Our Family 17

Chapter 2 – When You Were Young 33

Chapter 3 – Your Adolescent Years 51

Chapter 4 – Things You Learned About Life 87

Chapter 5 – Growing Older 125

Chapter 6 – Becoming a Dad 149

Letter from My Dad (Mark) 194

Post Journal Comments 196

Thoughts About the Topic of Dating (from Mark) 197

About CROP Ministries 200

About Faith 202

To Those Who Choose Not to Accept This Message 209

About the Authors 211

Acknowledgements (from Kaylyn)

My dad, Mark, guided me on this journey to publish this book. If he hadn't been the dad that I needed in my life, I would never have given him the journal to complete for me. I love you.

My mom, Jan, for always being there for everything that I've ever needed. Whether I was a minor, a single mom, or a married wife with two kids (your grandsons), you have always been a comfort and support for all of us. I love you.

My sons, Anthony and Cayden. I cannot measure the joy you bring me (not to mention all the laughter!) and I'm so blessed to be your mom. I can't wait to share this with you when you are old enough to understand. I love you both.

My birthmother, Sunni, and her entire family. I will always be thankful for your sacrifice in being willing to release your bloodline lineage (both Lizzy and me) to another family. Thank you for continuing to be an important part of our family. I love you all.

My sister, Elizabeth (Lizzy). We come from the same birth mother and were adopted into the same family. Nobody knows us like we know each other. I appreciate you for always supporting me, as I have supported you. I hope you can learn things from this book, just as I have. I love you.

Acknowledgements (from Mark)

This is the first book I've ever written. I hope it's not my last. But just in case, I want to thank everyone who has had an influence on this story being made.

First, my amazing wife Jan. My one and only wife of my life, married over 31 years as of this writing. She has always stood by me and believed in me, no matter the challenges in life. I love you! You will always be my #1 priority.

Kaylyn, my first-born daughter who gave me this journal. Without her actions, you would not be reading this right now. I love you! You will always be my Special-Special.

Elizabeth (Lizzy), my second-born daughter. You have played a huge role in my life in learning what it means to be a father, more than you know. I love you! You will always be my Sweet Little Papoose.

Dad & Mom (Richard & Katie) Martinez. Married to each other for over 68 years as of this writing. I observed through your words and actions what it means to be a sacrificial parent. I love you! I cannot imagine having lived my life without you both.

My sister Lynda, who showed me what it means to have a love relationship with God, in light of the hardships and challenges that life brings to us all. I love you! You have always looked out for your little brother.

My brother Steve, who, despite my descriptions of how he used to provoke me like a typical older brother does, truly does love me and has become a best friend. I love you! Thank you for your extreme generosity and the care that you have shown my family and me.

Bob Shank, founder of The Master's Program. You believed in me and brought me under your mentorship when I had no idea why God put me on this earth. You invested three years in me, despite my not knowing how to pay you, and as a result helped me to discover that CROP Ministries is what my life calling is.

Jeff Bennett, my spiritual brother, with whom we did deep dives into spiritual matters and discovery. We truly were iron sharpening iron, and you consistently provoked me to lean into my life calling once I discovered it.

Additional thanks goes to Suzanne Kearney, my proofreader. Beryl Glass, my book designer. Michael Ashley, my book advisor.

Preface

"Dad, Brook wanted me to say thank you for the lemonade you bought her at Panera," my daughter Lizzy told me. "It was no big deal," was my reply.

It was a Saturday afternoon, and I was working around the house. My 21-year-old daughter had stopped by to say hi when she was out and about with friends that day. It was shortly past lunchtime, and I hadn't had anything to eat. I asked them if they wanted to join me at Panera Bread for lunch, my treat. They said that they had just come from lunch and weren't hungry, but they would come with me to hang out for a bit. At the counter, I confirmed if there was anything I could get for them. They only asked for lemonade, a super easy treat.

"No, she really wanted me to be sure I told you how much she appreciated it. She kept asking me if I had told you yet," she continued. "What? What's the big deal? It was only lemonade," I said.

"You don't understand," Lizzy said. "Brook's dad died a couple years ago. She really misses him, and you treating her to lemonade reminded her of that."

Wow. Brook was the same age as Lizzy and her dad was gone. My heart broke for her. I then reflected on something.

When my two daughters, Lizzy, and Kaylyn, who is 2 ½ years older than Lizzy, were in junior high and high school, I always encouraged them to bring their friends to OUR house to hang out. I knew our house was a safe place for them and their friends. I wanted to know their friends and to get them to know both my wife and me. I wanted their friends to know that they were always welcome in our home, that they could relax and just be themselves, and that we were parents who were involved in our daughters' lives. As I came to know their friends, and my daughters would give me insight into their friends' households, this reality came to life: not all households, not all families were like ours. Not that ours was "better." This wasn't a competition or comparison, and I certainly had no illusions that all parents were involved in their children's lives like we were. What I came to realize was how MANY households did not have a mom or dad, or both, involved in their lives. How many of their friends were basically growing up on their own, learning about life the hard way. I learned how many of my daughters' friends had parents who were deceased, divorced, or disengaged. I knew that because so many of their friends had commented to our girls, "Wow, I wish I had parents like yours."

If you ask either of my two daughters, they will tell you how many of their friends I told, "Can we adopt you? Do you think your parents would let us adopt you?" If they all said yes, I would probably have two dozen kids by now, not just two!

As a dad, I've always had a real heart for people who grew up without a dad in their lives. It seems that many were physically present but were emotionally or mentally unavailable. I don't know what it's like growing up like that. As of this writing, my parents are each 90 years old and have been married for 68 years. They have always been, and continue to be, present and involved in my life. While they always encouraged and mentored me into becoming the man I am meant to be, they never overstepped their bounds in my life, my marriage, or my parenting. They were always a safe place that I could turn to whenever I needed life advice, and they almost always offered keen insight. I know our time on this earth together is quickly running out, and I often think in my mind, "What will it be like without my mom and dad here? What will be my thoughts? What will be my feelings?" The one thing that continues to play out in my mind, when that day comes, is that I might feel like I'm now on my own. Yes, I have a wonderful wife, great children, amazing grandchildren, and a whole lot of friends in my life. I won't be lonely, and I won't be alone. But I will be on my own. I won't have them there to lean into or fall back on during the storms that life will continue to bring. I'll have to figure it out. I'm so thankful that I feel well equipped by what they have sown into my life. Yet, I'll still be on my own.

Is that what it's like to not have a dad around? Is that the feeling that I can expect that countless others in this world are already living? Will it be something else? I know one day I will find out. But until then...

That is why I dedicate this writing to all the men and women, boys and girls, who don't have a dad in their lives. My hope, my prayer, is that somehow some of the writings contained in this journal will be an encouragement to everyone who reads it. Perhaps there might be some fatherly advice or wisdom that you never received that can be discovered within these pages. Will there be any insights that can help guide your thoughts, words, or actions, in order to help you enjoy a better and more fulfilling life? Here's what I know. We ALL have problems; we ALL have troubles in life. Granted, some more than others. However, while we experience brokenness through the relations we have, we can also find healing. May you find some sort of comfort and healing within the pages of this book.

NOTE: while I make several comments and statements in these pages to my daughter about God and Jesus, this is not intended to be a religious book. Rather, you are invited to have a glimpse into our lives and how God has shaped our beliefs, our values, and actions. It's up to each person to determine their own, and we respect your choices.

Definitions & Insights (from Mark)

I write about several things in this journal that, if you don't know me, you may not understand the context of what I have written. So, in light of that, let me define some things for you.

Adoption – my wife and I were unable to have children. We dealt with infertility, a very deep and dark time of our lives. Our family was formed because of the loving act of a young lady named Sunni, who gave birth to our two daughters. We had an open adoption, so our daughters know all about their birth family and our girls have a great relationship with them. Our adoption attorney told us that he has done thousands of adoptions in his career, and the nature of our relationship with the birth family is extremely rare. Our two daughters are Kaylyn, who gave me this journal, and Elizabeth, who goes by the name Lizzy.

CROP Ministries – CROP stands for Christian Rite of Passage. It is a faith-based teen mentorship program which I developed when my daughter, Kaylyn, was 12 years old. Throughout this journal I simply refer to the program as CROP. There is more about it at the end of the book.

Christianity – as I mention in the preface, this is not a book about religion or Christianity. It is a book about a dad answering his daughter's questions about his life, and their lives together. Our beliefs shape our values, and our values dictate our actions. It's up to you to determine your beliefs, and you are invited to see how ours have dictated our values and actions.

Munch & Gram – these are the names that my daughters call my parents, their grandparents. They call their grandparents on my wife's side Grandma and Grandpa.

The "Gang" – not a literal street gang. Rather, these were the couples that my mom and dad went to school with, hung out together, got married about the same time and all had us kids at about the same time. We would do all sorts of vacations together and, as a result, their kids and us became like cousins to one another.

— Chapter 1 —
ABOUT OUR FAMILY

What was the name of your mother and father? Where and when were they born?

My dad's name is Richard Martinez. He was born in Los Angeles, California in 1933. My mom's name is Catalina Martinez. Everyone knows her as "Katie," which is short for Catalina. She was born in Los Angeles, California in 1933. My dad's parents, my grandparents, were named Tony and Savina Martinez and they lived in Los Angeles. My mom's mom, my grandma, was named Trinidad and everyone called her Trini. My mom's dad, my grandpa, was killed when she was only seven years old, so she grew up without a dad.

Describe your mom, my grandmother. Did she have any funny habits?

Gram is amazing! She really had a hard life growing up. She is the middle born of five kids. When her dad died when she was seven, her mom was left as a single mom to five kids with no work skills. She wound up having a mental breakdown and was hospitalized in a mental institution. So, Gram wound up growing up in foster homes for eight years. I don't really know what it was like for her to grow up in foster homes, but I'm sure it must have been tough. I remember over the years her telling us stories of things that happened to her in which I said, "Wow, you probably should have died from that." I think I counted about 13 times that we think she should have died. Gram was also a very good athlete in school. In fact, in her senior year in high school, she was named Top Graduating Senior Girl of the school. The funny thing is that Munch (grandpa) was named Top Graduating Senior Boy of the school, and they barely knew each other! Gram was a great cook, loved parties and dancing, and everybody loved her. She had no enemies. Until she went into politics. She ran for California State Senate. Gram was always a very hard worker, and she earned both her bachelor's degree and master's degree while raising three kids. To me, Gram is the true Wonder Woman!

Describe your dad, my grandfather. Did he have any funny habits?

My dad, Richard Martinez, has always been a great influence in my life. He was (is) a great dad and I have many fond memories of him. He was an encourager, a coach, a fair disciplinarian, an adviser, and a lot of fun. As a kid/teen/adult, he was an excellent athlete. He played both football and baseball on his high school team and for the Army. He was smart with money (I did not get that knowledge from him) and a good businessman. After his time in the Army, where he served in Okinawa, Japan, he went to work for the telephone company. He worked his full career there and he retired when he was only 54 years old. You rarely heard him burp or fart like I always do. He loves football and we have so many great memories of watching football games together, both on TV and live games for USC and the Los Angeles Rams. My dad was the middle son of three boys and both his brothers have passed away. When I was maybe 10 or 11, he volunteered for the Big Brothers of America, where he played an adult male role model to a 14-year-old boy whose dad was killed in the Vietnam War. My dad always took us camping and we really loved to camp as kids. Like Gram, Munch was very involved in politics, and he ran for state Assembly and state Senate. My dad always worked very hard, and he sacrificed a lot for the family. I don't ever recall having any bad feelings for my dad, even when I would get spanked, because I always deserved it. He was also a great model to me on how a man should love his wife. He always adored my mom, and they would never argue in front of us kids. They have been married 68 years, since July 9th, 1955. I really love my dad and I've been unbelievably blessed to be his son.

Did you have any brothers or sisters, and did you want any? How did that change through time?

My older sister Lynda was born in 1957. She is the first born of us three kids. Her birth name is Linda, but she thought it would be cooler to spell it with a Y, so as a teenager she changed her name to Lynda. She is about three years older than me. My brother Steve was born in 1959. He is about 1 1/2 years older than me. Lynda and I used to fight terribly when we were young. It was both because she was bossy and because I had a certain amount of jealousy of her, because it always seemed to me that things always went well for her. It wasn't until I was much older that I found out about the struggles and pains she experienced in life. She became a born-again Christian believer as a young adult, and she played a big role in me coming to Christ and indirectly discipling me as a young believer. Steve was a typical older brother who could beat me at anything and would always pick on me just to make me angry, which he seemed to enjoy (kind of like Kaylyn and Elizabeth!). One day I finally had enough, and I punched my brother back so hard that he took a step back and pretty much said, "We cool." We have been best friends ever since. I took up running in high school, which was the first thing I was ever able to beat him in, so that became my sport. I was always happy that there were the three of us kids.

What was your favorite thing to do with your dad, my grandpa?

We did a lot of great things together that I have great memories of. We did Indian Guides together through the YMCA (no longer called Indian Guides). It was kind of like a Boy Scouting thing. We did lots of camping trips, played sports through the YMCA year-round, went on family camping trips to a place called Munz Lake. We played two-on-two football at Cal State LA with the boy that my dad was a Big Brother to, that I mentioned earlier. One of my favorite memories was when my brother and I would always offer to get my dad a cold beer when we were camping. Whoever got him a beer was allowed to open it for him and take a sip before handing it to him. My brother and I often took a very large sip, which is probably why, to this day, Steve and I like beer so much.

What's the best advice you got from your mom and dad?

My mom and dad have given me so much great advice throughout my life that there is no single best advice that I can think of. So, in no specific order, just as the memories come to mind:

"Walk in like you own the joint" (Dad). What he meant was that wherever you go, arrive with the confidence and assurance that you belong there. When you own it, you are in charge. (NOTE: back then, a gathering place was called "a joint," and this context does not refer to something you smoke. Just to be clear on this...)

"Eat what you can and leave the rest" (Mom). What she meant is that you don't have to stuff yourself at mealtime just to clean your plate. It's not good for you. Also, if you don't like something, you don't have to eat it. You're not going to starve.

"Go to college so that you don't have to start at the bottom and work your way up" (Dad). My dad graduated high school, went straight into the army, and then went to work for the telephone company. He started out climbing phone poles to run cabling and then moved up to management. He encouraged me to get an education so that I could start out my career at a higher level.

"It's important to know that when you pick a girl, you also pick her family" (Mom). This one needs no explanation.

My parents also constantly emphasized things like work hard, take care of your belongings, treat others well, guard your reputation, marriage takes work, never fight in front of the kids, spend time with your friends, love your family, be faithful, everyone does chores.

What is one thing I don't know about our family you think I should know now?

When I was young, in preteen and teen years, I didn't like kids. In fact, I really kind of disliked them. When I became an adult, I stopped disliking them, but I couldn't care less about them. When we got married, I figured I would have kids someday, but I felt no real urgency or desire. Then we found out we couldn't have kids. It was sad for me but devastating for Mom. It totally crushed her. From the time she was a little girl, all she wanted was to be a mom someday. It led her to a very dark place of depression, where she often considered suicide. When I found this out, I immediately got her into counseling. Eventually she was able to work through that, until we were able to pursue adoption as the way to have a family. After a few unsuccessful potential birth-mother matches, Mom and I each came to the conclusion that perhaps we weren't meant to have a family. So, we decided to call our adoption attorney to cancel our file. However, before we could call him, he called us and told us that another birth mother wanted to meet us. Her name is Sunni. We had talked about telling him no thank you, that we weren't interested, that we decided not to adopt after all. But I felt as if the Lord was telling me, "If you reject the meeting request, she may think you are rejecting her and rejecting the baby, and she might decide to abort instead." I knew I couldn't risk that happening, so we decided to take the meeting "as a courtesy" to Sunni. Mom and I went into the meeting with no interest in trying to woo Sunni to choose us. And then she asked me a question that I will never forget, and its impact on me. "Do you think you could love this child as much as if it was your own?" At that moment, I hadn't really understood the significance of that question and the deep impact it would have on her and me. For her,

> I would choose you both (to adopt) again 100 times out of 100.

she already had the love of a child (her first born child, your brother) that only a parent understands, and she loved you so much that she didn't want you to be robbed of the joy, love, satisfaction, and delight that a child brings to a parent. She wanted you to have all that you deserve. I remember my answer to her just as well. "I don't know. I don't have a child of my own, so I wouldn't know what to compare that with. But I'm sure if that were to happen, God would work that part out." And has He! Oh my, how He has. When you were born (and Lizzy too) the love I had for you girls was instant, complete, and without reservation. You were 100% mine, all mine (and Mom's too), and I never thought or felt there was even one ounce remaining to give to a biological child that I hadn't already given to you. The times of family arguments, disagreements, discipline, don't take any of that away. That's just part of being a family. But if you could line up 1,000 girls the same age as you and Lizzy, and I could choose any two to be my own, I would choose you both again 100 times out of 100. God really knew what He was doing when he put us together as a family!

Is there anything special about our family lineage? Do you know the origin of our family's name on both sides?

My mom knew much more about our family lineage than anyone else, and she shared it with me, but I don't remember. I believe our roots go back to Sonora, Mexico. However, here is a very interesting story. From 1910 to 1920, Mexico was enduring a Mexican uprising. One of the most prominent figures of the war was a Mexican general by the name of Pancho Villa. He was known to travel through small towns with his army and any able-bodied male who could hold a rifle was given the choice to join his army or be shot dead on the spot. A young 16-year-old boy decided to join the army, so he was taken away from his home and family. During one battle, the boy was shot and left for dead. When the battle was over, two guys were left behind to dig a large ditch to throw all the dead bodies in and then be covered up with dirt. While throwing bodies in, they heard moans and groans from someone inside the pit. One of the guys wanted to go in and find out who was still alive, but the other guy didn't. So the one guy climbed into the pit among all the dead and decaying bodies and pulled out a barely alive 16 year old. He left him with a local family who nursed him back to health. He then traveled to the United States for work. That young boy was Gram's dad, my grandfather. I never met him since he died when Gram was only seven years old.

Does our family have any special recipes that have been passed down?

Yes, of course! Our famous taco and salsa recipe. This was passed down to me by Gram. In addition, Gram also made me a little handwritten family recipe book for when I went away to college and included many of my favorite meals that she used to make for us, including:

Albondigas Soup

Enchilada Casserole

Katie Surprise

Potatoes, weenies, and cheese with tortillas

Unfortunately, I lost the recipe book and other than the taco dinner and salsa, I don't remember how to make the other dishes. Not to be outdone, Munch added his own recipe that he wrote in that book. He called it "The Bachelor's Recipe for Eating Every Night in Three Easy Steps."

#1. Get seven girlfriends that can cook.

#2. Have each one invite you over for dinner on a different night of the week.

#3. Enjoy!

How did your parents, my grandparents, meet? How did their parents, my great grandparents, meet?

Munch and Gram Martinez - They grew up together in an area of Los Angeles known as Palo Verde. They went to high school together at Lincoln High School, class of 1951. They knew of each other in school but didn't really hang out or were friends. They each eventually got a job at the telephone company. One day Munch went into the break room at the office and Gram was in there. A friend of Munch who worked with him said, "Hey, don't you know that girl? You should go ask her out." Since Munch didn't have a car at the time, but Gram did, he went and asked her out. They got married on July 9th, 1955, when they were each 22 years old!

Tony and Savina Martinez — Munch's parents. Also grew up in Palo Verde, Los Angeles. They knew each other from the neighborhood. I don't know how they started dating, but I think they got married when they were 19 years old.

How did you meet my mother? Describe your first encounter and your first date.

Oh, this is an easy one. I'll never forget it! I was in the single adults' group at Calvary Church in Santa Ana. I had been in the group for a while and there were not many prospects for me to choose from, despite there being a few hundred in the group. So, I asked who I felt was the best of the group out on a date. We went on a follow-up date after that. And then it happened... we were at Sunday school class for the young adults. I found that girl and I went over to sit next to her. After greeting each other, she said, "Oh, Mark, I'd like you to meet my friend Jan." Boing! Bonkers! OMG! Sitting on the other side of her, where I couldn't initially see her was your mom. Wow, what a hottie she was! She had these deep beautiful blue eyes, tan smooth skin, flowing blonde hair and a flawless smile. She told me later that she had a really bad migraine headache that day, so she wasn't feeling very pretty at all. After class was over, a whole bunch of guys rushed over to meet her. But I played it cool and waited for the right time. For several weeks afterwards, a group of us would go out to lunch after church, so we got to know each other a bit more. Then the singles class had a weekend retreat up in the mountains, about a 1 1/2 hours' drive away. I insisted with the carpool coordinator that Jan would ride in my car. We got to know each other pretty well on the drive up and we hung out a lot up there. When we drove back to the church after the retreat to get her car, I told her I'd like to see her and asked her if she would like to have lunch at Acapulco restaurant in Costa Mesa. She said yes. After our lunch date, which I refer to as the blur of the red nails, she was head over heels crazy about me and she wouldn't let me go unless I married her. (That last part's a lie.)

Did you ever experience love at first sight? Who was it with and how did you feel? What happened with this person?

So, as you get older, wiser, and more mature, you will realize there is no such thing as love at first sight. While it is a romantic notion with fairy tale type of inferences, love at first sight is a myth. While there truly is "attraction at first sight," or even "lust at first sight," there is not love. Why? Because we have to understand the definition of love. Contrary to popular belief, love is not a feeling. It's a decision. Can you imagine if love was only a feeling? You would fall out of love whenever you got upset with someone faster than you fell in love with them. While love does come with plenty of feeling attached, it truly is a decision to fall in love with someone. Why? Because of what the definition of love is. Love is patient. Love is kind. It is not jealous. It does not brag. It is not arrogant, it does not act disgracefully, does not seek its own benefit. It is not provoked. Does not keep an account of wrong suffered. It does not rejoice in unrighteousness but rejoices with truth. It keeps every confidence. It believes all things, hopes all things, endures all things. Love never fails. (1 Corinthians 13:4-8). So, it truly is impossible to apply all those attributes of love to someone at first sight.

Love is not a feeling, it's a decision.

What are some of the most interesting facts about our family?

I'm not sure what would be interesting, but here are a few:

- Munch ran for political office twice (state Assembly and state Senate).
- Gram ran for political office once (state Senate).
- Nina was one of the very first female police officers hired on the Los Angeles Police Department.
- I personally met and spoke to the 40th President of the United States, Ronald Reagan. My dad knew him when he was governor of California.
- Gram earned her bachelor's degree in education by going to college part time, working, and raising three young children. It took her seven years. She then got her Master's degree.
- As far as I know, you and Lizzy are the first children adopted into the Martinez or Osgood families.
- I love you girls more than you will ever know!

What was your all-time favorite holiday of us together as a family and why? Before you became a dad, what was your most memorable holiday and why?

I would certainly say Christmas for our family holiday. I always loved decorating our house in several bright, colorful lights that you could see from the end of the street. Mom always loved decorating the inside of the house, all the rooms of the house. You girls always got so excited helping to decorate the tree and seeing all the presents under the tree leading up to Christmas morning. Your huge eyes when you woke up and saw that there were even more presents than the night before are memories that I will never forget. I loved how excited both you and Lizzy would get when you would hand out presents after reading the names on the outside. I also loved how you would make fresh cinnamon rolls and hot chocolate for us to enjoy while we were opening the gifts. And who could forget our dogs Sasha, followed by Kayla as they would sniff round the bows and wrappers after they came off the gifts? Prior to being a dad, it may have been Thanksgiving, as I was able to eat a whole bunch of really good food. I used to like cooking a turkey on the grill using smoked wood chips to give the turkey a hickory flavor.

— Chapter 2 —
WHEN YOU WERE YOUNG

Where were you born? What was the first or earliest memory you have from your childhood?

I was born at Queen of Angels Hospital in Los Angeles, CA. The hospital is no longer there, and the building is now occupied by a church called The Dream Center. It's located just up the street from the original Tommy's Burger in LA, located on the corner of Beverly and Rampart. (Tommy's, that is). At the time, there was a small Mexican restaurant located across the street from Tommy's. That building is now used to store supplies for Tommy's, but my mom and dad were eating at that Mexican restaurant when my mom went into labor with me. It was a short drive up the street to the hospital from there. There were no ultrasounds back then to image the health or gender of the baby, and my parents were expecting that I would be born a girl. Since they were surprised that I was a boy, they had no name picked out for me. I was only known as "Baby Martinez" for a couple days or so. Finally, when the doctor that delivered me asked Munch and Gram if they had a name for me yet and they said no, the doctor said, "How about Mark?" My parents said "OK." So that's how I got my name.

What do you remember about your childhood home?

About nine months after I was born, my parents moved into a new home that they had built. The cost was $19,000, and the monthly mortgage payment was $90 per month. My parents still own that home today. It had three bedrooms and two bathrooms. It was a single-story home, but you had to walk up an outside flight of stairs to get into the house. I always recall the bedrooms being very large and the house seeming to be a big home, but in reality, it is very small by today's standards. The house is 1,288 square feet. Compare that to the Mission Viejo home you grew up in which is 2,400 square feet, almost twice the size. Our current home in Hayden is even larger at 2,900 square feet. I remember always playing in the backyard with my brother Steve. We played a lot of basketball because my dad installed a basketball hoop. Since the house was built on a hill, the backyard had three levels to it. In August of 1975, when I was still 14 years old, my parents bought the home in Arcadia where they still live. They bought it for $75,000, and their monthly mortgage payment was $425. That house has a pool and jacuzzi, so as a teenager I really loved that house!

What was your favorite TV show, song, and movie?

There were a whole bunch of TV shows that were my favorites. Most of them were comedies and some were action shows. Here's a list:

The Monkees. Batman. The Brady Bunch. The Partridge Family. The Addams Family. The Munster's. The Banana Splits. Run, Buddy, Run. Gilligan's Island. Sanford and Son. The Jeffersons. Good Times. Get Smart.

Cartoons I liked included:

Bugs Bunny. Roadrunner. Johnny Quest. Speed Racer. Gigantor. Spiderman. Dick Tracy.

Family dramas I liked included:

The Rifleman. Leave It to Beaver. Father Knows Best. Andy Griffith Show. Marcus Welby, MD. Adam-12. Emergency.

Sci-fi and action programs included:

The Twilight Zone. The Outer Limits. Charlie's Angels. One Step Beyond. The $6 Million Man.

The first song I remember liking was called "Brother Louie" by a group called Stories. I don't really know why I liked it, but the first vinyl record I ever bought was a 45 RPM of the song "(I've Been) Searching So Long" by Chicago. If you don't know what a 45 RPM record is, look it up!

Did anyone ever tease you about anything when you were young and what was it?

Yes, but I don't want to say. Eh, no. Not really. The only thing I can remember was I used to have a lot of hair. I would take a shower or bath at night, and I'd usually go to bed with wet hair. In the morning, I'd have bed head, where my hair was pushed up on the one side that I slept on, so one kid in grammar school would call me "Gumby Head." It never really bothered me much, because he was the only one who would call me that. He was one of those insecure kids who always talked so much and made fun of others before they could make fun of him. It's called "deflection." That is, deflect teasing away from you and put it on others. He was a weird kid and didn't have a lot of friends.

What did you want to be when you were little? In other words, what did you dream about becoming when you grew up?

Initially the answer to this question is pretty sad. I always noticed things around me, things that I thought were interesting, so I wanted to do those interesting things when I grew up. The things that I saw that I wanted to be when I grew up included a bus driver, a garbage collector, a construction site flag man, and a crossing guard. Fortunately, I grew out of that. My dad was a middle manager for the telephone company which was called "Pacific Telephone and Telegraph" at the time. He would sometimes go in to work on Saturday to catch up on work when the office was closed. I would beg him to let me go with him because I wanted to be with my dad. Plus, he would take me to some of his favorite places in Los Angeles for lunch! I remember great eateries such as Little Joe's (Italian), Paul's Kitchen (Chinese), Philippe's (French dip sandwiches), Tommy's Burger (best burgers in the world, as far as I'm concerned), and Clifton's Cafeteria. When I went to the office with my dad, for some reason I was mesmerized by a business office environment filled with desks, chairs, typewriters, trash cans, filing cabinets, telephones, and break rooms. I told my dad, "I want to do what you do when I grow up." As I mentioned previously, he then told me, "Go to college and study business. I didn't go to college, so I had to start at the bottom and work my way up. If you go to college, you can start in the middle and work your way up." So I determined then, when I was probably 12 years old, to go to college and study business. And I did.

What was the naughtiest thing you did as a child?

I did a lot of naughty things as a child. Our babysitter was so upset with my brother and me misbehaving that she locked us inside the bedroom. We popped out the screen of the window, tied sheets to the bedpost and climbed out the window. When she saw us outside, she chased us. We ran around the house, got back to the door before she did, and we locked her outside the house. She got really mad and when my mom came home, she quit. Other things I did included throwing rotten fruit at passing cars, stealing cigarettes from our next-door neighbor, stealing candy from the neighborhood market, pulling false fire alarms, damaging local gas station pumps, desecrating classrooms at the local college, terrorizing small animals, and more. (NOTE: from grown up Mark, I don't justify or condone ANY of those childhood behaviors. If my dad knew I did those things, he would have "stomped" me. That's the term that was used in our household which meant "being disciplined". He spanked us on the bottom, and rightly so because I always deserved it, but he never beat me or my siblings.)

What was your imagination like? Did you ever play pretend and what did you pretend to be?

My imagination was probably pretty similar to most young boys. I always played Army and I pretended I was an Army man. I also pretended I was a football player, a race car driver, an astronaut, and a rock musician. I really liked girls at a young age, so I always imagined what it would be like kissing them. I was too nervous and didn't have enough self-confidence to actually do it, so I never kissed my first girl until I was 14. And then it was lights out! I kissed every girl that would let me put lips on her. I learned right away that I liked it, and so I did it as much as I could. I know, now it's the part where you go "Ewww!" if you haven't done so already.

What did you want most as a child that your mom and dad never gave you?

I can't think of anything. Although we weren't rich, nor was I spoiled, my parents always worked very hard to provide us with things we needed. I never really felt like we lacked anything or that I wanted something that they could not or would not provide. The only thing that kind of came to mind is when I was a teenager. I had just gotten my driver's license and the neighbor down the street was selling a car. It was a tricked-out muscle car, lifted in the back with mag wheels and a super-fast, souped-up engine. It was what we referred to as a "hot rod." I begged my dad to buy it for me, but in his wisdom, he said no. He knew I would have raced it and crashed it.

What were you afraid of when you were little (the dark, monsters under the bed, etc.) and how did your mom and dad comfort you?

There were a few things that I was afraid of when I was young at various ages, but I don't recall ever telling my mom or dad. Not that I couldn't, or that there were any barriers to talking with them. Rather, I just didn't think to tell them. The funny thing is that every one of us has fears. Not just when we are little, but throughout our lives. Fears never go away, they just change. Not that we always live in fear of something. They come and they go, and they can be absent for long periods of time. Yet something new may come up that we never faced before, or a bad memory may pop up in a present situation, and the fear comes back. There are some common fears that most males and most females share. Most females fear, "Am I beautiful? Am I desired by someone? Will someone fight for me and protect me?" Most males fear, "Am I strong? Am I any good to those around me? Do I have what it takes?" I remember reading about this in John Eldredge's book Wild at Heart. These may be considered self-doubts rather than fears, but they are common, and they are real. Some of the fears I had when I was younger included:

Fear of the dark. Fear of something bad under the bed. Fear of dying. Fear of my parents dying. Fear of being abducted by space aliens. Fear of dying before having sex.

What do you miss from your childhood?

It's interesting. We miss things that we once took for granted and didn't realize that we valued them until they are lost. I'm not sure if there is anything that I actually miss. As a child, there is no responsibility for having to work, pay for things, etc. Of course, there were school and household chores. So in a sense, there is loss of limited personal responsibility. However, I prefer to be able to work and to manage money and belongings. All the things I enjoyed in my childhood I feel I still have. Good health, sports, exercise, my parents. A warm bed and home to live in. Friends, a sharp mind, love. However, there are so many things that I now have that I didn't have as a child that are so important to me now: Salvation in Jesus. A wonderful wife. Wonderful children. Wonderful grandchildren. I guess I have learned not to look to the past too long for something that I can no longer have. Rather, only look to the past to enjoy fond memories, but be in the present to be grateful and to be content with all that I have today.

> **Be in the present and grateful for all that you have today.**

Did you have a favorite family vacation, road trip or outing that you remember fondly from childhood?

Oh yes. There were numerous family trips, vacations and outings that we went on that I have fond memories of. My favorite was the place called Munz Lake. It was a campsite north of Los Angeles near Castaic Lake, Hughes Lake, and Elizabeth Lake, off of Lake Hughes Rd. and the 5 Freeway. My family's friends, "The Gang," used to camp there all the time. We would swim, fish, catch frogs, collect soda bottles, dance to both live bands and a coin-operated jukebox, and go on hikes. We would also do beach outings at Zuma Beach in LA and Huntington Beach in Orange County. We went on summer trips to Las Vegas and would stay in hotel and motel rooms. We often went to Rosarito Beach in Mexico, just South of Tijuana, where we rented a beach house with The Gang. We would swim in the ocean, go to bull fights, shop for curios, eat carnitas dinners and real churros for dessert. My dad, my brother, and I were also very involved in the YMCA, which originally stood for Young Men's Christian Association. It became "politically correct" later on, and changed their identity to just "The Y." We did sports through the YMCA all year around and there were numerous camping trips that we did with just the guys. I used to really love going camping and I regret that I did not take you girls camping more often when you were young.

What rules or chores did your parents give you that you swore you'd never give your own children (including me)?

I wouldn't say there were any chores that I had to do that I despised so much that I swore I would never have my kids do. Despite nearly every kid hating to do chores, I always knew it was critical that every person who lived in a home has an obligation for its upkeep. I remember always complaining about having to do chores and trying to come up with different ways to delay having to start them. For example, "I'll do it at commercial time... I'll do it when this TV program is over... I'll do it after I go to the bathroom." I did chores such as mowing the lawn, raking leaves, taking out the trash, cleaning my room, doing dishes, vacuuming, dusting and things like that. The one thing I disliked the most, for some reason, was hand watering the yard. I don't know why I disliked it back then. I just remembered that I did. But now I actually enjoy it (when we were in Mission Viejo, not here in Idaho, since our current home does not need any hand watering). I think I came to like it when we were in Mission Viejo because I would be listening to my favorite music with my ear buds while I was watering. It made the time go by faster.

What was the town/city like that you grew up in? What was there to do there?

From the age of 1 – 14, I grew up in Los Angeles, the eastern part of LA, right next to the Alhambra border. In the summer, before turning 15, we moved to Arcadia. Today I usually tell people I grew up in Arcadia because Arcadia is so much nicer than LA. In LA, we lived just a few short blocks from Cal State LA, a major California University. I almost always felt safe there. I always played with my friends in the streets all around the neighborhood. We would ride our bikes all over the place. We played football and basketball. My dad mounted a basketball hoop and backboard onto the edge of the roof in our backyard so my brother and I would play basketball and shoot hoops for hours both day and night. There was and still is a local neighborhood grocery store named "Valley Foods" that we would always walk to for snacks, candy, and soda. We always called it "Yuki's" because the Japanese couple that owned it were named Frank and Yuki, and it was Yuki who was always working in the store. By the way, that is also where my brother taught me how to steal candy. We lived in a part of LA where there was gang activity, but the section we lived in never really had any problems. However, that's why we moved to Arcadia to ensure we kept our distance from any encroaching gang activity.

What childhood experiences did you have that you wish I would have gotten to experience?

Freedom and safety. When I was a kid, we would wake up on weekends during the summers and leave (after doing our chores), and not come back until after dark. We didn't really have concerns or issues with abductions, kidnapping, trafficking, etc. Granted, those things did happen, but it was nothing like it is now. Back then, kids would walk to school with no issues. Nowadays, it's like you never want to let your kids out of your sight. Back then, there was no fear of growing up. Now, it seems, people are afraid of where the world is going and what it's turning into. Back then, it didn't seem like the color of your skin was a big deal, like it is today. Maybe I was naive back then, or perhaps I'm jaded now. Or even a bit of both. But it seems like much of innocence has been lost. Maybe you don't see it and thank God if you don't. It would be so much better for you if you saw the world more so like through the eyes of a child rather than those of a battle-worn old man. Ultimately, my hope is in Jesus. This temporary world that we live in is nothing compared to the hope and the promise of a life eternal with Jesus.

Did you ever dress up for Halloween, pull any pranks, or did anyone ever scare you? What ghost stories and urban legends haunted your community?

Halloween. I always dressed up, went trick-or-treating, and got lots of candy. I don't remember all the characters I dressed up as. Some of them were planned ahead, and other ones were kind of last minute. Some of the characters that I remember included: an army man, a hobo, a fat man, Batman, a ghost (just cut out two eye holes in a white bed sheet and put it over my head... Gram was not too happy when she found out).

Pranks. The top prank we would do is to ditch someone whenever we would go somewhere. For example, whenever we would go to Cal State LA to play on the campus, we would pick someone to ditch. Whenever that person would be distracted (e.g., they would go to the bathroom, stand in line at the cafeteria to buy something, etc.), the rest of us would run away and hide from them so that they would be left alone to wander. Usually, we would pick the youngest person. Whenever it was with Clifford, Bruce, and my brother, I was the youngest one, so I typically got ditched a lot.

Ghost stories. The most famous one in Mexican folklore is La Llorona. This is the wailing lady that drowned her children at the request of her lover, only to be later abandoned by him, leaving her alone with the guilt of killing her children. Her spirit flies through the night, haunting all who see her.

What was the scariest moment from your childhood?

OK, not sure what the scariest moment was, so I'll throw a few of them out there that could be contenders. In no particular order:

- The time I almost drowned in the ocean when I was 12 or 13 because I got caught in a riptide and was washed out into the ocean. I was able to swim parallel to the shore and then back in, but it took the last ounce of energy.

- The time I got hit by a car while riding my bike and I nearly got run over by the car when I hit the asphalt. I remember landing halfway under the car as it was skidding, and I rolled over to my left side as the rear wheel passed right behind me.

- I was playing in the gym at Cal State LA, swinging on the gymnastics rings when I slipped and landed on my back. I got the wind knocked out of me and I couldn't breathe. I thought I was going to die, so I jumped up and started running home because if I was going to die, I wanted to die at home.

- When I was a teen and just started driving, I crashed the family station wagon.

- In Catholic grammar school, every 3rd grade boy was required to serve as an altar boy during church services (Mass). When it was my turn, I was afraid that I would forget how to do something or that I would do it wrong, so I started crying and my mom got me excused from serving. I never got scheduled again.

- My brother and I crashed on a bicycle going downhill really fast.

- I got attacked and mauled by a police-trained German shepherd dog when I was about four years old, and I almost died.

What's the biggest difference between your childhood and mine?

From a parent/adult perspective, I think about the nature of the world that we are now living in and the direction it is going in. The reality is that every generation of parents, for centuries upon centuries, thinks that the world that our kids are growing up in is worse than the one we grew up in. In large part, that is due to parents being more aware of world events than our kids are. You know, as a parent you want to provide the best for your children while also protecting them from all the dangers and evil that the world brings. The older you get, the more things you see that just are not right. However, here's the most important thing that I hope I can communicate to you here: we are not meant for this world. That is, this world, and our human bodies, will pass away. It's just a matter of time before all that we know ceases to exist. But our spirits will live forever. God intended us to live with Him for all eternity. This begins the moment we accept Jesus Christ as our Lord and Savior. When this happens, we begin our eternal life with God, part of it now in this body on this earth, and the rest of it in the manner He has in store for us. With this eternal perspective, this should recalibrate our focus from the problems that we can face each day to the peace, joy, and hope that God brings us. The more we learn to focus on Him, the better things in "our" world seem to be.

What was the best moment from your childhood?

I really had to think about this one since I had so many really great moments that I can remember. Lots of great memories on family vacations, sports accomplishments, playing with friends, holidays, gifts received, etc. However, the moment that kept coming back to mind over and over again, when I was thinking about this question, was something unexpected that I walked into when I wasn't a child. I was in my late teens or early 20s. I was living with Munch and Gram still, and I was getting ready to head out on a Friday night. I walked into the family room to tell them, "I'm on my way out," and Munch was sitting in his chair enjoying a martini and Gram was sitting on the floor by his feet with an arm on each other. When I walked in, they both looked up at me with smiles on their faces and tears welled up in their eyes. It caught me by surprise, and I asked them if everything was OK. Gram looked at me and said, "It's just so wonderful to be in love." Wow! That rocked me. How my mom and dad can be married for so many years and still have such a deep love for each other. This validated to me that marriage still works, despite all the divorces going on. What a great infusion of peace and security for a child to know that their parents' marriage is solid and safe. That moment left a deep impression on me and has carried me through my own relationship in my marriage with Mom.

— Chapter 3 —
Your Adolescent Years

What did you hate/love the most about growing up?

When I was a kid, the thing I hated most was thinking I was never going to grow up. I thought I was always going to be a kid. I remember thinking that my parents were born as adults, that they never were kids, and that they had no idea what it's like being a kid. My childhood and adolescence were really good, and they're filled with many really great memories. I'm very grateful that my family was intact. My parents were faithfully married to each other, and we attended very good schools. I always had friends. I played sports and was better than average and I had a pretty good work ethic. From the time I was 12 years old, I had a job and I earned money, so I'd never felt broke and hopeless. The one thing I never learned was the discipline of saving the money that I had earned. I wish I had done a much better job at that. I'm still a spender and not a saver, which is why I'm still working while several of my peers my age have already retired. Of course, most kids don't like doing chores, and I was no different. I did them anyways, but I wouldn't say I hated them. I always loved my mom's cooking. It seems that everything she made was delicious. I can't recall if there was anything she made that I didn't like. If so, she probably just didn't make it again. Oh, I almost forgot. My brother always picked on me and would get me all worked up. I would get so frustrated and angry, and I would start to cry. Finally, one day I had enough, and I punched him really hard. From that day forward, we became best friends.

What was the hardest lesson for you to learn as you grew up?

I would say learning not to be selfish and jealous. Being the baby of the family, I would say I got a little bit spoiled and often got what I wanted. When you get used to that, you often feel you are the center of the universe, that everything should revolve around you. When you don't get your way, you get upset. Don't get me wrong here. I was not a spoiled brat or an obnoxious kid like perhaps others that you may have seen or known. In fact, it seems in our nature that we are all selfish to some extent. You don't have to teach a child to say, "me, me, mine, mine!" It just comes naturally. For me, it seems the process of learning not to be selfish is lifelong. Now regarding jealousy. I learned that hard lesson in high school. When I was a junior in high school, I took a P.E. class in running. I got very good and very fast, and I set a record that had never been accomplished in that class. The P.E. teacher made a big deal out of it, and this seemed to catch the eye of a very pretty girl in class. We started dating, even though I always felt she was way out of my league. Lots of other guys liked her, but she dated me. Anytime a guy would talk to her, even the ones that were just friends, I would get super jealous and quiz her about who she was talking to and why. She finally had enough of it, and she dumped me. I really deserved it. But I learned the hard lesson that nothing good comes out of jealousy.

Who was your first crush and what happened with them?

Well, does my third-grade teacher, Mrs. Edwards, count? Probably not. So that would then be Carol K. in 6th grade. Carol had a twin sister, Carmen. People often had a hard time telling them apart. But I could. Carol had fair skin, long and straight brunette hair, and beautiful blue eyes. I always had a weakness for girls with blue eyes. (Note: See your mom for reference.) I would always look at Carol and watch her whenever I could without being creepy about it. In fact, one year for Christmas, my sister was going to give me a silver wrist bracelet with my name engraved on top. I asked her to engrave Carol's name on the underside where only I could see it and knew that it was there. Of course, she said, "Ooh, who's Carol?" She was in 9th grade by this time (my sister), so she was all into preteen crushes and romance. Because I didn't have the same level of self-confidence that I have now, and I always was a bit shy back then, I never busted a move on her and let her know how I felt. I don't know whatever happened to her. As I recall, her family left that school prior to 7th grade, and I never saw her again. PS. There is a picture of her in my Mark Martinez 1985 family photo album that Gram put together for me. Look at my 6th grade class group picture and you'll find her there.

Who was your first kiss? Where was it and what was it like?

Oh wow, talk about personal. Are you sure you really want to hear this? You won't get grossed out? Oh well, here it goes. My first kiss was with a girl named Joyce. It wasn't supposed to be with her. It was supposed to be with a girl named Cindy. Cindy and I are the same age, and when we were about 13 or 14 years old, we developed a crush on each other. We were talking on the phone extensively with one another and we would write letters back and forth. No, not emails or text messages. Actual handwritten letters. I eventually got enough courage to hold her hand and we both really liked it. But I was too nervous to kiss her, despite me knowing that she wanted me to. Then one summer, we all took a large-group, family road trip to San Jose for a friends quinceañera. One of the girls that was in her group of girl attendants was Joyce. I really liked girls a lot, and I learned to be a pretty good flirt early on. I started flirting with Joyce whenever Cindy was not around. Joyce responded. Then on the night of the quinceañera, as it was about to end, knowing that we were all leaving the next day, I met Joyce out at the back of the building, and I knew this was my moment. So, I leaned in and kissed her, and she received it really well. I knew she wanted me to. It was really nice. But there was a problem. Cindy's younger sister busted us. She went and told Cindy and boy, was she mad. Cindy had been waiting a long time for me to kiss her. Yet I went and kissed someone else. Oh well, I guess it was all a warmup because I eventually started kissing Cindy. You're welcome.

Did you have a high school sweetheart? Spill the beans...

OK, you asked. This is going to sound like bragging, but it's not:

- 9th grade — 4 sweethearts (Cindy, Pamela, Donna, ???)
- 10th grade — 2 sweethearts (Pam, Carol)
- 11th grade — 1 sweetheart (Lisa)
- 12th grade — 2 sweethearts (Marie and Jan — they were sisters)

There were also several other girls that I knew wanted to date me, but I was not interested. The ones I recall were Debbie, Helen, Laura, Diane, Paula, Christine, Natalie, Fran, and Lisa. The one you really want me to spill the beans on was Lisa B. in 11th grade. She's the one I talked about earlier about the lesson I learned on jealousy. I really believed she was out of my league, which is what led to the jealousy. One thing I learned was that she was a born-again Christian. Me being raised Catholic; I didn't know what that was. I remember her telling me that we can never get married because she was Christian, and I was Catholic. To start, I don't know how or where the idea of marriage came from. Heck, I was only in 11th grade! But it did make me curious because I didn't know what that was. In hindsight, I would say she was one of the very first persons among many who planted the seeds of a personal relationship with Christ on my spiritual journey to salvation at my age of 26. The other thing about her was that she had blonde hair and blue eyes and spoke perfectly fluent Spanish. Made me look like a bad Mexican. Lisa was the one real sweetheart in my life that I swore I would leave any other woman if she happened to come back into my life. But then I met your mom. She has been, is, and always will be my number one sweetheart for all my life! Mark loves Jan!

What/who influenced your style and taste as a teenager?

Well, believe it or not, it was Nina's high school boyfriend, Danny. He was one of those guys that seemed to have everything going for him. Good looking, great hair, artistic, musical talent. In fact, he was the guy in high school that a lot of girls wanted to date. So whatever fashion that Nina would wear, the other girls in high school would copy her to catch his attention. Then the guys would copy what Danny was wearing to catch the girls' attention. They actually set fashion trends. Then there was David Cassidy, a musician who also played on a TV series called The Partridge Family. He was a teen heartthrob, so I often emulated his style as well. Did it work? Was I successful in following Danny's and David Cassidy's style and taste? See previous question and answer.

Who was your celebrity crush and where did you first see them?

It was a tie between Farrah Fawcett and Cheryl Tiegs. They were both supermodels and the crush/fantasy of every teenage boy at the time. They each had a bedroom wall poster that made them extremely famous worldwide. But as I think about it, the celebrity crush I had before them was Susan Dey. She was a television actress on a program called "The Partridge Family." They were a traveling musical band, and she played the role of Laurie Partridge, backup vocalist and keyboardist. The thing that all three of these celebrity crushes had in common was they had blue eyes, fair and tanned skin, and light shiny hair. Now you know why when I first saw your mom, I said, "Wow-za!"

Did you have any favorite classes or subjects? Do you remember a particular teacher?

Yes, for sure! My favorite subject has always been English, and my favorite teacher was Mrs. Edwards in 3rd grade. I always remember her as being very kind and helpful. However, the thing I remember most about her is at a parent-teacher conference. I remember sitting with her and my parents at the meeting and she told my parents, "Mark is reading at a 6th grade level." I remember thinking, "Wow, if I'm in 3rd grade reading at a 6th grade level, then when I'm in 6th grade I will be reading at a 9th grade level!" This really motivated me to become a very strong reader and I really enjoy reading to this day.

> I'm amazed to this day how such a simple statement from a teacher set such a strong course in my life.

I'm amazed to this day how such a simple statement from a teacher set such a strong course in my life. Here's a funny story, though. My mom was a substitute teacher at my school. One time she was a substitute in my class. She gave us an assignment to work on and several of us students had questions. There was a small line waiting their turn to ask a question and I thought, since I was her son, that I should get a special privilege. So, I went to the front of the line when she was talking to another kid, and I started yelling at her. "Hey, hey, hey!" I didn't know how to address her. Mom? Teacher? Mrs. Martinez? So, she turned to me in front of the class and said to me, "My name is not 'Hey,' it's Mrs. Martinez. Now go sit down." All the kids went "Oooh!" I was embarrassed and my mom felt really bad about having to do that.

Did you ever get into trouble at school? What did you do and what was the punishment?

OK, I came up with a couple more. When I was in 4th grade, it was a really hot day, and the school had no air conditioning. I was at a Catholic school and my teacher was a nun. The class was really unruly that day and I could tell she had pretty much had it with us kids. Just then, a small dog walked into the classroom, as the door was open in order to help cool off the room. All the kids went crazy and started yelling for the dog to come to them. "Come here, doggy." Unfortunately for me, the teacher was standing right next to my seat. So, when I called for the dog too, she turned and slapped me across the face. The classroom fell into a stunned silence as the teacher screamed out, "Don't call for that dog. Don't anyone call for that dog!" Needless to say, I was super embarrassed to be slapped in front of my friends. Another time, as a high school senior, it was a tradition that the entire senior class ditch school for a day. You know, you did it too. All the teachers and staff knew it was going to happen along with the seniors, so we just had to have our parents sign a note that we were truant for that day.

What was your favorite fad from your generation? What fad was the most embarrassing when you look back?

Bell Bottom jeans. Platform shoes. Smiley face. Superball. Tang. Troll dolls. Twister. Yo-Yo's. Bicycle banana seats. Mood rings. Peace symbol. Disco. Puka shells. Mexican jumping beans. Pet rocks. Star Wars. Streaking. Jogging. Waterbeds. Roller skating. Clackers. Pong. Hacky sack. Rubik's cube. Boom box. Walkman. Look them up.

None of them were embarrassing when I look back. Everything I ever did was super cool, and they still are. Except streaking. I never did that.

What was your most memorable school event (dance, game, etc.), and what made it so memorable?

Well, I think perhaps one of the things that stands out most, that everyone remembers from their teenage years, is what/who they remember as their first true love. I mentioned Lisa before. Our first date was miniature golf. Our second date was a movie where we held hands for the first time. Our third date was Disneyland. That one was the magical, memorable event. That's the one where we held hands, hugged a lot, and kissed a lot. Talk about the Magic Kingdom! Remember, this is the girl that I felt was way out of my league and now she's romancing with me! We were there throughout the day and stayed there at night until it closed at about 10:00 PM. Walking around, holding hands, hugging, arms around each other, kissing your dream girl. Wow! To be clear, no hanky-panky took place. Just a memorable day and evening of romance.

P.S. No hanky-panky took place!

What kind of student were you and did you belong to any groups or cliques?

I was a pretty good student. If I recall correctly, I graduated with a 3.4 GPA on a scale of 4.0. We did not have GPAs above 4.0 back then like there are today. While I struggled a bit with geometry and algebra, I was pretty good in all other subjects. In 10th grade I joined an on-campus service club called the Junior Exchange Club. It was the high school version of the Arcadia Exchange Club. I was in it for three years and was president of the club my senior year.

I developed a growth problem in my knees because I was growing too fast. As a result, I was grounded from all sports from 7th through 11th grade. I had not been a part of any sports teams during that time. When I got cleared to play sports at the start of 11th grade, I took a jogging class as my PE elective so that I could get in shape for football in my senior year. Football was always my number one favorite sport. I wound up repeating the jogging class for my PE elective my entire junior year in high school, and I got pretty good at it. Our final exam was running 3 miles for time, and I was the first student in the PE class at the school to ever run under 18 minutes for three miles. This led me to transition from football to cross country/track and field in my senior year. My hangout group became both the Junior Exchange Club and the distance runners in my senior year.

What does your yearbook say about you?

From the guys: You're a cool dude, lots of fun, great memories, etc.

From the girls: To a handsome guy, stone fox, wish you would have asked me out, etc.

PS - I pretty much just made all that up. I don't recall what my yearbook said about me, and I don't know if I even have it anymore to see what it would say.

What was your greatest school accomplishment?

I'm not sure what I would consider my greatest accomplishment, but there were several things that I was proud of and grateful for. The fact that we moved to Arcadia in the summer before my sophomore year of high school and starting the first day of school knowing absolutely nobody other than my brother, but graduating my senior year with a LOT of friends was a really good thing. Being a minority in a predominantly white school without ever being picked on or demeaned. I was never bullied or ridiculed. I had a different girlfriend every year. Being voted by a very wide margin as the president of the Junior Exchange club my senior year. Being the first person to break 18 minutes for three miles in the jogging class. Winning my first one-mile race in track and field on the JV team with my mom there to watch it. Being moved up to the varsity team right after and competing against guys in my first year of track that had been running for four to seven years. Getting the track scholarship to community college to help pay for my education expenses while still being able to compete. Working a job throughout high school and college while still balancing my academics and athletics. Learning to deal with grief through the unexpected and tragic death of Colleen C. More on that later.

Who was the biggest influence on your life growing up and was it positive or negative?

Not sure if I had a single biggest influence. I wound up having many people who influenced my life in many different ways. If I had to choose a single one, though, it would probably be my mom. I spent more time with her than with anyone else. She clothed me, fed me, changed me, bathed me. She taught me how to use the toilet, brush my teeth, clean my ears, and make my bed. As I got older, she taught me how to cook, clean, sew, do laundry, iron, and vacuum. She taught me manners, gratitude, perseverance, and the value of educating myself. She cleaned up my wounds when I had an accident. She held me when I cried, and she even rescued me from the jaws of a wild German shepherd that attacked me and nearly took my life. My mom was patient with me, put up a lot with me, and she never made me feel like a disappointment or burden. I remember that

> My mom was definitely the biggest influence on my life.

my sister, brother, and I each liked something different for lunch. Rather than making the same thing for all of us, which would have taken less time, she valued our uniqueness and made a different lunch based on our preferences. I remember when I was in school and I had homework projects due, or term papers that needed to be typed, I would go to my mom and ask for help. She would ask, "When is it due?" I would say, "Tomorrow?" She would be up all night finishing my work for me while I fell asleep. My mom never let me down. So yes, now that I think about it, my mom was definitely the biggest influence on my life.

Did you ever have any friends your parents didn't like?

I really don't think I did. My parents always taught me how to be a good judge of character. Not that I could ever recall us sitting down and having a discussion about it. But perhaps more so, as a result of seeing them as they chose their friends, who they hung around with and who they avoided. I recall certain friends of Lynda and Steve that they had concerns about, but I cannot think of any of mine.

And then there was Lisa.

Not Lisa B., the high school sweetheart I wrote about before. I'm talking Lisa F., the girl I almost married that nobody liked. This girl was just a bad fit for me. There is no other way to say it. I dated her because she was a Christian, she played softball, and I thought she was cute. I asked her to marry me because I felt sorry for her, and I wanted to rescue her. Absolutely a wrong reason to marry someone. My parents were against it, my sister was against it, most of my friends were against it, and I knew in my gut that it was the wrong thing to do. Fortunately, I came to my senses before it was too late, and I backed out of the wedding and ended the relationship. Was it hard? For sure. Even though I knew it was the right thing to do, it was still very hard. But keep in mind that oftentimes the right decision is the hardest one to make.

What was the hardest thing you ever had to tell your parents as a teenager?

The hardest thing I feel I ever had to tell them was not as a teenager, but when I was in my early 20s and I was in college at San Diego State. I had joined a business fraternity called Delta Sigma Pi. When you joined a fraternity your first semester, you were referred to as a "Pledge." That means during your pledge period you are being evaluated by the "Active" members in the chapter, those that have previously completed their Pledge period, and you are learning the ways of the fraternity. Once a year during the end of the school year (usually in May), the chapter would put on a season-ending banquet. They would rent a large hotel banquet room, have a formal sit-down dinner, do awards and recognition, have a slide show of events throughout the year, and have a dance with a DJ spinning songs. When I was told about this banquet, I was told I could invite whomever I wanted. So, I called my mom and dad, told them about the banquet, gave them the date and invited them. They were so excited to come and to finally see all about this Delta Sigma Pi fraternity that I had been telling them about. When I was asked by my fraternity brothers if I had invited anyone to the banquet, I said, "Yes, my parents." They said, "Uh, we meant a date. You could invite a date. Nobody has ever invited their parents before." I thought that was wrong since it was because of our parents that we were even in college. I had to call my parents back and tell them the story, then uninvite them. I knew they were disappointed, and it crushed my heart. The next year I was on the committee to change the rules and parents were invited for the first time. The banquet was a HUGE success, and I was happy they could be there.

Did you ever experiment with anything? What was it and what happened?

Do you mean like ... drugs? Tobacco? Illegal substances for minors? Of course! But nothing big. Our next-door neighbor (Clifford and Bruce's grandpa) was a smoker. Whenever he wasn't around, I would go over there and try a cigarette. I only did that a couple of times because I didn't like it, but as a kid you think you look all grown up when you smoke a cigarette. It's not true. You really look stupid while thinking you look cool. In 9th grade, I went to a friend's house to hang out. We then went to some other guy's house where there were a bunch of people, but I didn't know anyone. They were smoking weed and were passing around a joint (this time, I'm not talking about the "walk in like you own the joint" kind of joint). Eventually it came to me. Thinking that I had to smoke it, even though I had no curiosity or desire, I took a puff and I immediately started coughing up a lung. When you don't know how to smoke pot, you wind up taking smoke into your lungs and you feel like you just breathed in fire. Of course, when someone else starts coughing and choking, it's really funny. But when it's you that feels like you're going to pass out and die, it's not. And then there was the time my girlfriend, Lisa B., as a sophomore, went to the high school prom with a guy friend of hers that was a senior, and I know he really liked her, but she only saw him as a friend. I told her it was OK for her to go, just to prove that I was not jealous or mad. But boy, was I mad and jealous! I don't have room here to write about what happened that night, but wow!

EPILOGUE

OK, this part was not in the original journal that I wrote for you because I was out of space, but I'm going to explain it now.

When my girlfriend went to prom with that senior guy that really liked her, and she was a sophomore, I was very jealous and upset. Only seniors were allowed, unless they invited a sophomore or junior. I was at home that evening and my good friend Clifford called me and asked me what I was doing. I told him what happened and how angry I was. He said, "I'll be right over." He came over and picked me up and drove us up into the mountains nearby to a popular lookout point that was famous for couples making out or friends getting high. He then reached behind the seat of his truck and pulled out a cigar box. He opened it up and there was a bunch of weed and a bong. He told me, "This will make you feel better." Other than that time I spoke about earlier, when I was 14 years old and I was passed a joint at a party, I had never really smoked pot before. I didn't know how to use a bong. Clifford took a hit off of it to show me how to do it. He took another hit to make sure I understood. He then passed it to me. We were both already laughing. I laughed really hard before I could even take a hit and all the pot blew out of the bowl all over the inside of the truck. That really made us laugh even more. He set up another bowl for me and I took a hit and that one seemed to be OK. I don't remember how many hits I was taking that night, but I do remember starting to feel really good, really relaxed, really happy. I forgot all about Lisa. I remember my cheeks started hurting because I felt like I was smiling constantly. I looked at the side-view mirror on my side and I saw this big grin on my face that just wouldn't leave. After talking and listening to music, I finally said, "Man, I'm really hungry!" Clifford said, "You've got the munchies, man." So, we drove down the mountain and we went to a local Denny's. I remember ordering a ton of food. But while we were waiting for the food to arrive, I started feeling pretty sick. I went to the restroom and puked my guts out. Clifford came to check in on me and was slapping me on the back, asking, "Are you OK, buddy?" It just made things worse. I finally cleared out my stomach and went back to the table and all the food was there. But suddenly, I was no longer hungry. I don't think I ate anything. Then we went home, and I don't remember what happened after that.

PS — I do NOT recommend smoking pot or taking drugs. It can put you on a path that leads to nowhere. I cannot change my past experiences, and even though the story sounded funny and enjoyable at the time (it was), we could have really run into trouble driving down that mountain.

What is your biggest regret of your teenage years?

I can't think of any big regrets I have from my teenage years. Despite the stories I mentioned earlier, I never became a smoker, alcoholic, drug user, sex addict or rebellious. I obeyed my parents, did well in school, worked for money, was nice to most people. I did OK in sports, didn't really have any enemies and pretty much enjoyed life. I was never depressed, never suicidal, never self-absorbed. I had good physical and mental health. There are a couple things that do come to mind, despite being somewhat trivial. They didn't have any impact on my life long-term. The first is that I wish I had a bit more self-confidence to pursue some girls that I thought were very pretty and would have liked to date, but I felt intimidated. I never had sex with any girls when I was a teenager. (I know, "Oh, gross! I just threw up a little in my mouth!"). However, I did love "the thrill of the hunt." That is, the process of flirting with a girl, getting her to be interested in me, go on a date, hold hands, hugging and kissing. That's as far as I would go, but I really enjoyed that. The second thing was that I wish I would have worked and tried harder in sports. If I made a greater commitment to practice, seeking advice from my coaches on how to excel, and building self-discipline (eating, sleeping, rest, mental toughness, pushing my limits), I know I would have done better in competitions.

Where did you hang out as a teenager and what did you do?

In my high school years in Arcadia, I had a few groups I hung out with.

Group 1. My brother, Chris R., Tony H., Mike R. We were the Mexican guys that hung out, drove around town, raced cars, and were mischievous but never really got into trouble (although we should have).

Group 2. Kent C., Chris B., Rick L. We would play cards, listen to records, hang out at the park, and play racquetball.

Group 3. A bunch of people that I ran track and cross country with in my senior year. We would run a lot and have parties.

Group 4. The Junior Exchange Club. We would have meetings, do service projects, have social gatherings, and pool parties.

Group 5. My girlfriends. We would go out on dates to the movies, miniature golf, the mall, the beach, dancing, and we would kiss a whole lot.

Group 5 was my favorite group.

Did you ever think about college and where did you want to go? Why did you want to go there, and did you get to go? Why or why not?

Yes, I knew I wanted to go to college since I was about 12 years old. My dad placed that thought into my mind at an early age. I remember going in to work with him sometimes on Saturdays. I was mesmerized by the office environment that he worked in, and I knew I wanted to do the same thing as he was doing once I grew up. He told me then that I needed to go to college so that I could have the best chance possible of working my way up the corporate ladder and becoming successful. I decided at that time I would go to college. I never questioned it. I thought I would start out right away at a four-year university right out of high school. However, I started competing in track and field and in cross country in my senior year and I was good enough to compete at the junior college level, but not at the university level. So, I went to Citrus College in Azusa, CA first. I earned my AA degree there while running and I then transferred to San Diego State. When I graduated Citrus, I was ready to go away and start living on my own, but I didn't want to go so far away that I couldn't get home quickly if I wanted to. For me, that meant either San Jose or San Diego. I'm so glad I chose San Diego. I really loved my time and experiences there. Good education, good friends, good memories. I remember one time late in my junior year, my mom telling me, "You know, I realize college is very hard, and Dad and I always expected you to go. But I don't think we ever asked if you wanted to go. So if it's too much for you and you don't want to finish, that's OK with us." I responded, "What are you talking about? Of course, I want to go to college. I'm going to finish no matter what. But thanks for asking."

> I'm going to finish no matter what.

When you got older, how did what you want to be change from when you were younger? What is the dream you wanted most for your life?

When I was younger, my aspirations were very low. I wanted to be a bus driver, a garbage collector, a gas station attendant, a construction site flag man. Basically, the things that I saw in my daily world were the things that I wanted to be. Unlike some kids who wanted to be an astronaut, a policeman, fireman, or a doctor, I wanted to be the kind of worker who was actually working. That is, people who I saw were busy doing their job. Thankfully for me and for my parents, I grew out of that, since my personality now would never have been a good fit for that type of work. As mentioned earlier, I knew I wanted to be involved in sales and business. I never wavered from that dream. I've never felt like I should have been a... you fill in the blank. The only time that did change was in 2002, when I became an ordained pastor at Mission Hills Church in Mission Viejo. At that time, I thought my career would be to forever transition into full time ministry. I would leave the business world behind. It turns out God had different plans for me. He had me there at that moment for His specific purpose, for His specified time, and that was it. I'm grateful for His plan in hindsight, but I didn't understand it at the time.

What was the first car you wanted and why?

The first car I wanted, I was never going to get. One of the neighborhood kids a couple years older than me in high school had a hot rod for sale. A "hot rod" is the term we used for a souped-up custom car modified to drive fast. I don't recall the model of the car, but it was a green Chevy, raised in the back, with fat black-wall tires. I think it was an 8-cylinder dual-cam 357 engine. That baby roared when you started it up and the sound of the engine idle would beg for somebody to race it. I just got my driver's license, and I had just started to work, but I didn't have enough money saved up yet to purchase the car. I pleaded with my dad to purchase the car for me, and I promised to pay him back. But like most dads he knew better than that. He knew I wouldn't just use the car for transportation to and from school. Or to go to work. Or to go to the store. He knew I would use that car for what it was modified to do... to race. So in his wisdom, he didn't buy that car for me. He let me borrow the family station wagon, which I crashed by driving too fast. He eventually bought me a four-cylinder poop brown Toyota Corolla lift-back with stick shift. Clearly not a chick magnet, but it got me to and from school and work and I never raced or crashed that car.

How did growing up in your decade differ from mine, and what was the biggest difference?

The biggest difference, clearly, is the internet and smartphones. When I grew up, the world was limited to where you lived, where you traveled, what you picked up by watching the nightly news. Now you can literally visit any place in the world, see what's happening in real time, and learn about its history without ever leaving your home. When I grew up, learning came from people who taught you and books you read. Now learning comes from asking Siri or Alexa a question and trusting that her answer is correct. When I grew up, a friend was someone you hung out with and spent time together. Now, a "friend" is someone you connect to via online profiles, whether or not you ever met them. It seems to me that people were kinder, harder working, and more respectful of others when I grew up than they seem to be now. There didn't seem to be such division among people as it seems now. People seemed to value family, take more personal responsibility, and not demonize others that they disagree with like they do now. Personal values differ quite a bit now versus then. Back then, most people that lived together were married. Most childbirths were to married couples. There weren't as many divorces. Clearly, not as many abortions. Most people did not live on government welfare. A much larger percentage of the population were Christian/Catholic and went to church. I'm not making value judgments here. Rather, I'm just comparing how different things were in my decade of growing up compared to yours. All these changes in only one generation.

Did you ever rebel? If so, what did you do?

Define rebel. What do you mean by that? Well, since you are not here to help me understand the question, I'll go ahead and offer a definition. While some young people "rebel" against their parents through constant arguing, fighting, and doing everything opposite of what the parent tells them to do, I would say I never did that. I think I respected my parents too much to try to get in their face and tell them how it's going to be. Besides, if I ever tried, I know my dad would stomp me! The extent of my "rebellion" would have simply been me doing things that I know they would not have approved of. For example, stealing candy from the local market. Using profanity and telling crude jokes. Drinking alcohol when I was underage. Getting a fake ID when I was 19 so that I could purchase booze. Driving drunk. Cheating on tests. All things that I don't advise anyone should ever do.

> I respected my parents too much to get in their face.

Did you have an after-school job or did you want one? Tell me more about it.

Yes, I had several after-school jobs. My first job was being a paper boy. I would deliver the newspapers on my bike to the neighborhood. I started that when I was 12 years old and continued on until age 14. We then moved to Arcadia at age 14 and I didn't work again until age 16 when I got a job at Santa Teresita Hospital in Monrovia. I was an assistant to the brain surgeon... eh, no. I worked in the area of kitchen food service. The cooks would prepare the dinner plates for the hospital patients. We would deliver the huge food carts with all the dinner trays to each floor of the hospital. We would then pick up the carts with all the trays, scrape off all the food and trash, wash and stack all the trays and dishes, clean the carts, and then clean the whole kitchen. In my later high school and early college years, I got a summer job working for the telephone company where my dad worked. During the school year in my first couple years of college, I also worked at a music record store. When I went away to university, I worked in a restaurant, first as a bus boy and then as a waiter. As you can see, I always worked while also going to school and running track.

Did any world events or politics affect you growing up? How did you cope?

There were some MAJOR world events that took place when I was growing up. Several ones took place when I was younger, and they didn't affect me because I did not understand them at the time. These include the assassination of President John F. Kennedy, his brother Robert Kennedy, and Martin Luther King Jr. Other events included the Vietnam War, man landing on the moon, and Watergate. The things that I do remember having an impact on me were the 1976 Summer Olympics, the boycott of the 1980 Summer Olympics, the 1980 Winter Olympics, and the 1984 Summer Olympics. I also remember the recession of the 1980s, fuel shortages and gas lines, and the evacuation of the Vietnamese to the US at the end of the Vietnam War. The Vietnamese evacuees were probably the biggest impact that I noticed had an effect. Not on me directly, but in what I observed. At that time, I recall Southern California as being fairly racially segregated. For the most part, you had blacks, whites, Hispanics, and Asians settled into their own areas, their own neighborhoods. Following the airlift of all the Vietnamese, and them being spread out all across the US, that's when I first noticed racial integration. Back then it was very rare to see racially integrated couples and families. Nowadays it is very common.

What was your favorite summer vacation? How did you usually spend summers?

As I mentioned earlier, Munz Lake was one of my favorite vacation places. If you asked any of us kids from "The Gang," we would all say that Munz Lake was one of our favorite vacation spots. Some of my other favorite summer vacation spots that I enjoyed were road trips. We went to Las Vegas lots of times. The City of Lights was always a great time. We also took lots of road trips to national parks such as the Grand Canyon, Yellowstone, Carlsbad Caverns, Yosemite, Hoover Dam, Zion National Park, Petrified Forest, Bryce Canyon, Death Valley, Arches National Park, and Meteor Crater. As you can see, we did a lot of outdoor vacations. I don't recall us vacationing very much at tropical resorts, island life, or beach destinations. We did take several vacations to the mountains to play in the snow. As teenagers we learned to snow ski and we really enjoyed doing that as well.

What was your most embarrassing moment in high school and how did you survive it?

Hmm. I probably had more embarrassing moments in grammar school and after high school than I actually did in high school. So let me share some quick events that I can recall throughout my younger years.

- As a child I got caught stealing a 5-cent candy bar from our local store. When the owner said to pay for the candy or else she would tell my mom, I pulled out a $1.00 bill from my pocket. She said, "Why are you stealing a 5-cent candy when you have a dollar?" I didn't have a good answer.

- The time in 6th grade when I initiated a fight because a kid made a derogatory comment about my mom, but I lost the fight.

- The time in 7th grade, I asked a blonde girl if I could walk her home and carry her books for her and she said, "Eww, no!"

- My first day of 10th grade at Arcadia High School, where I didn't know a single person and I felt like a total foreigner.

- In my senior year in high school, I qualified to run in the Pacific League championships for the mile. I was really scared because I knew all the other seven guys were faster than me. I started out way too fast. I had a huge lead halfway through the race, then I completely ran out of gas, and I finished dead last in front of hundreds of people in the stands.

- Same thing happened again in college when I qualified for the Southern California championships. Except this time my dad was there. That was the only race I recall him ever coming to.

What wild and crazy ideas did you have for after high school that you never pursued?

I had a lot of ideas that I never pursued. I still do. My mind comes up with all kinds of creative and crazy ideas that I never pursue. So here are a few of them, in no real order.

- Stand-up comedian. I have written so many hysterical jokes, in my mind. I'm sure if I ever write them down and put them in order, I can put together a really funny routine.

- Music stand in movie theater lobby. Prior to music streaming, I had the idea of selling LPs, CDs, and cassettes in movie theater lobbies that were playing movies with really great soundtracks. The idea came to me after seeing the movie "Amadeus" in 1984.

- In the late 80s, I covered a sales territory that included Seattle. I noticed all the coffee shops that people would go out and hang around in. I remember thinking, "We don't really have coffee shops like that in California. I should open one." I didn't.

- In the early 90s, I visited my brother after he moved to Connecticut. On Sunday morning, we went to the local bagel shop to get breakfast and to buy bagels to take home for the week. I remember thinking, "We don't have any bagel shops in California. I should open one." I didn't.

- I thought of providing a very expensive service where someone could contract with me that if they died unexpectedly, I would have legal authority to go wherever they told me to confiscate everything that they secretly were hiding so that it would not be discovered by their family.

Did you play sports, instruments, or participate in school activities? What did you like and what were you good at?

Oh yes, I always LOVED playing sports and doing school activities. My favorite sports were football and basketball. My brother and I played all the time. I was actually pretty good at them. I was terrible in baseball, though. When I hit 7th grade, I developed constant pain in my knees. It turns out I had a growth problem where my bones grew too fast for the supporting ligaments. The doctor grounded me from doing any sports for four years. I was finally released to do sports again when I entered 11th grade. Since my first love was playing football and I was pretty out of shape, I took a jogging class that year to build up my strength and endurance. I actually got pretty good at running, too. In fact, I was the first person at the high school that took the jogging PE class to run 3 miles in less than 18 minutes. The summer before 12th grade, I was in football camp and the coaches had us all run one mile around the track (4 laps) for time in football cleats. By the time I finished my 4 laps, I passed every other guy once and passed half the guys twice while running the mile in 5 minutes and 47 seconds (5:47). My football coach pulled me aside and said that I'm not a football player, I'm a runner. I converted to cross country/ track and field for my senior year. I also competed at Citrus College for two years. I tinkered around on the piano a little bit. I was a very good disco dancer. I got elected to the Junior Exchange Club as President my senior year. In college I was a very active member of Delta Sigma Pi, a professional business fraternity.

If you were going to pack a time capsule in high school for your future child to open, what do you think you would have packed for me to see and why?

Gosh, I'm not sure I can remember what was popular at the time. I'm thinking that some things I would have packed are:

- Disco records. Because disco ruled at the time.
- Cassette tapes and vinyl LPs. There were no CDs or streaming. 8-Track tapes, too.
- Polaroid photos. It was fun taking a picture and watching it develop.
- A pet rock. A weird but totally genius invention.
- A Farrah Fawcett poster. Almost every boy had one, even me.
- Something from Star Wars. The first movie came out during high school.
- Bell bottom pants. They were the fad and are popular again.
- Platform shoes. High fashion and they make everyone taller.
- A rock concert ticket. Lots of live shows that I saw.
- Chia pet. Like the pet rock, a stupid but genius fad.
- A yellow happy face button and T-shirt. It was the 70s, man!
- My driver's license and student ASB card from high school.
- A copy of the movie "Grease," starring Olivia Newton-John and John Travolta.
- A bag of Reese's Pieces. They were invented in 1978.
- A copy of the first Van Halen album.
- A Cabbage Patch Kid.

Did you graduate high school? If so, how was it and what was the highlight of graduating?

Yes, for sure. I graduated in 1978 and I believe there were about 847 kids in my graduating class. A big class, for sure. Arcadia High School in Arcadia, CA. Not sure if I can think of a highlight of graduating. Some various things that I remember:

- It was a hot day, and I wore a 3-piece suit with cap and gown.
- During the ceremony, somebody launched a bottle rocket towards the stage, and it flew right over the head of the valedictorian.
- I was both happy to be finished with high school, but also sad that this stage of my life was coming to a close.
- I didn't have a girlfriend at graduation, so that was a bummer.
- I got all kinds of graduation gifts.
- The summer after I graduated (1979), we took a family trip to Europe and visited 7 countries. That was really cool.
- We moved to Arcadia the summer before 10th grade. In the three years of high school, I only went to the Santa Anita racetrack once, despite only living half a mile away.
- I went to every single formal dance throughout high school, with the exception of prom in 10th grade, as sophomores were not allowed to go to prom unless they were invited by an upperclassman.

Did you dream about getting married and what kind of wedding you'd have? Who did you think you'd marry and what kind of wedding did you want?

Oh yes, I knew I wanted to get married someday. I love the companionship and excitement of having a love relationship. However, I never felt the urgency to get married when I was young. In fact, I remember when I was 15 years old telling my mom that I did not want to get married until I was 30. She said, "Where did that come from?" I told her, "I don't know. I think there are too many things that I would like to do, and it seems it would be easier for me to do them if I wasn't married." My mom then said, "Well then I'm going to teach you to cook, clean, do laundry, sew, and wash dishes, because I'm not going to continue to do all that for you until you get married at 30!" (Note: I got married the month before I turned 32.) I was always attracted to Caucasian women. I like the blue/green eyes, blonde/brunette hair, and fair/tan skin look. I figured I would marry one of those, even though my grandma Savina Martinez (Munch's mom) wanted me to marry a "nice Mexican girl." I thought at my wedding, I would play and sing the song "Wedding Song (There Is Love)" by Noel Paul Stookey to my wife as part of the ceremony. The only problem is that I can't play guitar and I sing terribly.

What's the most important thing you learned in school that actually helped you in the real world?

I'm not really sure if any one specific thing comes to mind. I learned a lot of things in school that are extremely helpful to me today, such as math, reading, writing, spelling, grammar, etc. I'm not sure if things like history, geography, science, or art help me in any ways in the real world other than for trivia or clear curiosity. Certainly, sports helped in terms of discipline, teamwork, competition, failure, etc. If I were to look back on lessons learned in school, I would say the most important thing in life for me was the importance of people and relationships. Meeting new people, talking to them, finding common interests, including them, treating them with respect, understanding each other's uniqueness. I recall in grammar school feeling a little bad because I wasn't being invited to certain parties. It occurred to me that if I wanted to HAVE a friend, I needed to BE a friend, so I started inviting people to my house and they would in turn invite me to theirs. I also learned that most people are followers, and they are looking for leaders to follow. To be a leader, it just starts with standing up in a group and speaking up. People will follow. [I have a story from college about that that I'll have to tell you.]

> If I wanted to have a friend, I needed to be a friend.

What other hopes and dreams did you have for your life?

There were LOTS of hopes and dreams that I had for my life. I wanted to travel a lot internationally. I wanted to obtain unlimited access passes to the Summer Olympics every four years, no matter where they were held. I want to go to Israel and tour the Holy Land. I wanted to be financially independent. In fact, when I was 30 years old, I actually sat down for about half a day and wrote out all the things I wanted to accomplish in my life. I covered areas of personal health, family, career, finances, spiritual, and recreation. I was really happy with what I wrote out, because I felt that if I accomplished everything on that list, then I could say that I had lived a fulfilled life. However, there were two major things that I did not do, which resulted in me not accomplishing very much on that list. First, I did not keep that list in front of me on a regular basis. Without reviewing the list, I lost my way on where I wanted to go. With no map showing the way, I wound up taking whichever road that life placed before me. I lost sight of my hopes and dreams. The second mistake I made was that I never put together a plan on what I needed to do in order to meet those dreams. As a result, I did not do the daily/weekly/monthly disciplines that were needed to accomplish those dreams. Hopes without a plan will only remain dreams and never become reality. I don't even know where that list is that I wrote out when I was 30. Perhaps I will find it again one day. The sad thing is that I will probably be on my deathbed one day and think about wasted opportunities. However, I will be confident that I did not live a wasted life. I have Jesus and I have my family. I'm filled!

— Chapter 4 —
THINGS YOU LEARNED ABOUT LIFE

Where did your life take an unexpected turn, and how did it happen?

Without a doubt, on Thursday, February 26th, 1987, at 1:13 PM. That is the day and time that the truth of God, the reality of Jesus, the forgiveness of sin, and the adoption into God's family took place. Yet I didn't understand any of that at the time. All that I really understood was that I had finally found the spiritual truth that I was looking for. You see, leading up to that time, I felt everything was going great in my life. I had a college education, I was working a good job, making good money. I lived in a great home, drove a nice sports car, and had nice clothes. I had good health, a great family, lots of friends, and a nice girlfriend. You could say that I had everything that most people would want for a full life. Yet something was missing. An inner peace. A purpose, a meaning for life. I longed for something that wasn't physical. It had to be something spiritual. So I started researching world religions. I wanted to find truth. Along the way, I came to learn that truth was not some thing, it was some one. That person is Jesus Christ. "I am the way, I am the truth, I am the life" (John 14:6). Through all my reading, all my research, I came to know the truth of the Bible, of God, of Jesus Christ on that February day. I didn't understand all the elements of what I just described or what I know now. I only understood that the Bible was truth, Jesus is truth, and the meaning and purpose for my life would be found there.

What's the most important thing you learned about relationships?

We all have relationships, and we all need relationships. Mankind was not designed to live alone. There are some relationships you have no choice over (the family you were born into, who you work with or went to school with, the neighbors you live next to). There are other relationships you have full choice over (your friends, church, who you hang around with, and where you spend your time). The important thing is choosing the kind of relationships that help to make you better and in turn help to make them better. Keep in mind that throughout life you will have times where two or more relationships that you have chosen will come into conflict with one another. You will need to choose which one to keep and which one to distance yourself from. I suggest reviewing the relationship pyramid that I put together in CROP to help you out.

Is there a secret or key to happiness?

Love the Lord with all your heart. Don't depend on your own understanding. In all your ways, acknowledge Him and He will direct your life. Remember this: happiness depends on you choosing to be happy, no matter what. If happiness is dependent on other people or your circumstances, why are some very wealthy, young, beautiful, talented people with lots of friends so miserable, whereas simple, poor, and uneducated people can be happy? The difference is the attitude they choose and their relationship with the Lord. Only the Lord can bring you a deep sense of happiness and contentment no matter what your situation is in life.

What was the hardest period of your life and why?

Colleen C. Without a doubt. It was a hard, terrible, emotional part of my life that I wasn't prepared for. I was in high school. You will recall that I mentioned earlier that I liked girls a lot and I had several "sweethearts" during those years. There was a time in my senior year when I wasn't dating anyone when I met Colleen. She was pretty, super sweet and very nice. We met up two or three times at a party and some school events. I knew that I liked her and that she liked me. I met her mom, her dad, her brother, and her best friend. Things were going well. The next step was for us to start dating. Then I got a phone call that really rocked my world. Colleen had been hit by a car while riding her bicycle, and she was in the ICU. I'll never forget that day. Her mom and dad met me outside the hospital room to prepare me for what I was about to see. Although there was no physical damage to her face or body, she was brain dead. A machine was keeping her alive by forcing her body to breathe and to keep her heart pumping and blood circulating. But without the machine, her brain wasn't able to cause the heart to pump. She would never recover. The sound of the breathing machine, the sight of her body artificially rising and lowering from the forced air, the smell of the hospital room. I nearly passed out. This was my first, up-close, and personal experience with death. I wasn't prepared for it. I didn't know how to handle it. Thankfully, I received a lot of support and encouragement through the process. That experience left an impact on my life, and I still think of her on occasion (not to take anything away from Mom). I still have a picture of Colleen.

Was having a family as rewarding as you thought it would be?

It was better. Much better. And it's hard. I feel like I grew up in a very loving family. My mom and dad stayed married and committed to one another. We went to private school for most of our lives. There wasn't much drama and there was no abuse. We were never hungry and never homeless. I always knew I wanted to get married and to have kids. I just didn't want to do it too early. I didn't think I would get married until I was at least 30 and I married one month short of my 32nd birthday. Since I was one of three kids growing up and I liked that number, I wanted to have three or four kids. Since your mom and I couldn't have our own biological kids, the Lord blessed us through the adoption of two wonderful girls, amazingly from the same birth mother. I'll always remember the day we brought you home from the hospital. You were fed, you were changed, you were warm, and we put you in your crib to sleep. Mom and I looked at each other and said, "Well, what do we do now?" We both said, "I don't know." We stood there, just staring at you while you slept. Parenting tips can be learned from others, but parenting can only be learned by going through it yourself. Yes, there are a lot of challenges, struggles, failures, and disappointments of being a family as you go along. Yet the love and the rewards are so worth it. I would do it again 100 times out of 100.

> The love and rewards are so worth it.

What life challenges were the most difficult for you?

One of the things that I have struggled with, and still do to this day, is thinking that I'm not good enough, that I don't have what it takes to be successful. I know things that I'm really good at, the things that come naturally to me and that I'm gifted at. Every person is gifted in some things. I know my potential. Yet I oftentimes feel that I come up way short of my potential. I'm not really sure where that self-limiting belief comes from and how to overcome it. All I can think of is remembering things from my past, where I lost in a sports competition, was defeated in an event, failed at something I tried, or performed poorly in something. It seemed that despite the shortcomings, everything turned out OK. Nothing really terrible happened. I didn't suffer a great loss. I sometimes think that in order to be successful, great effort is required (which it is), and that achieving average is easier and acceptable. In my mind, I fear that one day I'll look back on my life when it's too late to attempt something great and to leave a legacy, and I will be filled with regret. I'll feel like I wasted the opportunities that were given to me. Time does not wait for me to figure it out and get my act together. The older I get, the shorter my window of opportunity. I have a greater sense of urgency. Each day presents a new chance for me. I pray that I won't miss it.

Was there any area of your life you neglected that you wish you hadn't?

Yes, for sure. Money management. While it may seem that Mom and I are doing well financially, we truly are struggling. Of course, we have a nice home, two nice cars, nice furnishings and belongings. We never miss a meal, and it seems we have disposable income to spend money on whatever we want. In reality, we are having a tough time financially. All the money I had saved up and put away for retirement was wiped out during the housing crisis in 2008 to 2010. We are nowhere near being able to retire. My problem has been with my money management. I've never established a spending plan (budget), never exercised self-control and discipline. I used credit and borrowing irresponsibly. I never paid myself first whenever I earned money and then left that money alone for the future. That is why in the lesson I wrote on money for CROP, I know what I'm talking about. It's because what I advise in that CROP lesson is everything that I didn't do. I see the stress that this puts on Mom. She feels she needs to work lots of billable hours in order to provide for us when my business is down. I often joke that I'll retire when I'm dead, but that's no joke for Mom. It wears her out. My advice is that you exercise the disciplines needed to not wind up in the same situation that I put us in. Spend less than you make. Save and invest now for your future. Pay the Lord what is due to Him first and pay yourself second. Don't take money from your retirement to pay a creditor. They won't care if you're broke, but you and your family will care.

What life event brought you the most emotional pain?

I would say the church division and split that I went through in 2003 to 2004. In August of 2002, I left my 16 year business career in computer systems, and I went on full-time staff as Director of Outreach and Evangelism. I had been volunteering at church, taking on leadership positions, and was voted onto the elder board. It seemed the more I served, the more I felt God's pleasure. When my pastor asked if I would be willing to go on full-time paid staff, I believed this was where God wanted me to be and that this would become my full-time career for the rest of my life. I obtained my pastoral ordination, which meant I was able to legally marry people as well as perform baptisms and funeral services. I came on staff in August of 2002. In December of that year, a very ugly letter was written and signed by about 26 members of the congregation that were what I referred to as "old guard discontents." They laid many false and misleading accusations against our senior pastor. For the next 18 months, I was right in the middle of two groups of people that were fighting against each other: those that wanted to fire the pastor and those that wanted to keep him. The 26 members that wanted to fire him grew to about 80. Our congregation had 904 members at the time. The infighting got really ugly. Relationships were broken, people left the church, staff members quit, and I saw it all unfold before me. I was the secretary of the elder board at the time, so I was in all the meetings and taking all the notes. I knew the truth, so I defended the pastor and his reputation. The mob then turned on me as well, with one person even telling Mom that my head should be cut off and delivered on a silver platter.

What mistake did you make that you'd never want your children to repeat?

There are several of them that I think are important to discuss and could be life lessons for my children:

1. Accept the Lord Jesus as Savior much earlier in life and remain close to Him throughout your life. I didn't do this until I was 26 years old, which means many of the decisions I had made up until then were selfish decisions that were harmful to me and harmful to others.

2. Never drive drunk or while under the influence of mind-altering substances. I did that numerous times between the ages of 19 through 25, and it was only by God's grace that I was never arrested, crashed, injured myself and others, or killed someone.

3. Learn to manage money better. Even though I taught so many of these financial literacy classes, I've done a poor job in making, saving, investing, and spending money.

4. Maintain sexual purity for your spouse only. Prior to accepting Christ at the age of 26, I was either promiscuous or unfaithful if I was dating someone. When you do that, you imprint those images and memories on your brain, and they can come back to visit you. This robs you of the full amount of joy and satisfaction that God has intended for you and your spouse alone.

Did you ever experience peer pressure? What happened and how did you handle it?

Yes. I'm certain that everyone experiences peer pressure at times throughout their lives. Sometimes you resist it, and sometimes you succumb to it. The earliest peer pressure, I recall, was when my brother and our two friends pressured me to steal candy from our local store. At age 14, I was pressured to join a gang, but I resisted and told them no. When I was on staff at church, I was pressured to join that group that laid claims against our pastor, but I resisted and said no after investigating their claims. I'm certain there were several other peer pressure moments. Here's what I've learned. If I'm uncertain whether or not I should do something, doubt is its own answer. If I doubt if I should do something, then don't do it.

> Doubt is it's own answer.

What do you think is the root of all evil and why?

The Bible says, "The love of money is the root of all kinds of evil" (1 Timothy 6:10). To be clear, money is not the root, but the love of money is. Why? Because when we love money, it's because of selfish reasons. I believe that the three core temptations of mankind are pleasure, power, and possessions. These are the three things that cause us to sin, and they are all selfish desires. The more we receive, the more we tend to want. And how do we get more money? When we love money and place it as our highest desire, we can lose the opportunity to be content with what we have. This robs us of "today" joy. And what do we do with the gain of added wealth and riches? We buy more pleasure, power, and possessions. All selfish things.

What did you learn about becoming a dad and parent?

The biggest and most important thing I learned about becoming a dad is understanding so much more of how God feels about me. When we were awaiting your birth, I did not fully feel or grasp the concept of being a dad. I had confident expectation that it would be a pretty cool thing to have a family by having a baby. Since Mom and I were unable to have kids, we did not really have the experience of seeing or feeling you grow prior to birth. Rather, for me it kind of felt like we had ordered a package that we were waiting to have delivered. I hadn't developed a love feeling or emotional attachment. All I knew was that there was going to be a new human that I was going to be responsible for, and that there would be some things that I was going to have to sacrifice (pleasure, power, and possessions). Then you were born. And then I saw you for the very first time. You were only 20 minutes old. It was instant. My life was transformed in a flash. I was so filled with love, joy, total happiness. I felt attached to you, despite you not yet being able to be attached to me. And it struck me: if I had this much love for you, in spite of my imperfection, how much more does God have for me when He is the only one capable of perfect love? I wanted to give you everything good, just like God. I wanted to protect you from everything bad, just like God. When you grew older and would disobey me, I felt sad, just like God. My personal love for God grew immensely in the shadow of my love for you, until His love grew larger than the shadow.

What was the scariest thing about raising a child?

I think for most parents, the scariest thing about raising a child is messing up. Am I doing it right? Can I do better? Am I missing anything? Is my discipline too hard or too easy? Will I do anything that is going to screw them up forever? Most parents will say things like this, "This kid didn't come with a user manual." Yes, it's true. Parenting is something you learn on the job. That's why it's so important that as a parent, you take the role seriously. Be a student of the job, a lifelong learner. Read books, go to seminars, sign up for workshops. Watch videos, talk to others, and get advice from other parents. Don't be afraid to try things out and be willing to fail. Also recognize that every kid is unique. Despite having the same DNA and coming from the same womb as their siblings, they will have different interests and will respond differently to things such as rewards and consequences. The hard part is adjusting to each child differently to help them to be the best person that they can be while still being as fair as possible to everyone. Remember, each child is a part of the family, not the centerpiece. If you allow a child to be the central focus of the family, you will inhibit their ability to launch well and be independent. If you raise your children, you can spoil your grandchildren. If you spoil your children, you will raise your grandchildren. It seems in today's environment, one of the other scary things is just keeping your kids alive. With deadly drugs such as fentanyl., impaired driving, risk-taking, online bullying, depression, and suicide being so prevalent, it is critical to have kids understand that they have value. They were created for a reason. God wants them here to fulfill their life calling while the devil wants to kill and destroy their lives. Yes, life can be challenging, and children can be stressful. But it's worth the living.

What did you learn about true friendships?

True friendships are those in which you help each other to be better. It's when you truly enjoy being around each other and you look forward to spending time together. Friendships are not just between two or more unrelated people. Friendships can be between parents, siblings, cousins, and spouses. Friendships provide excitement when trying new things, and enjoyment with old things, and challenge you to be the best person possible. They help us learn and grow, challenge us when we are off base, rejoice with us in victory and accomplishment, and stand with us during difficulties and defeat. Here are some insights on how to determine if someone is a true friend:

- A friend helps you, not hurts you.
- A friend lifts you up, not puts you down.
- A friend is happy for you, not jealous of you when you have something that they don't.
- A friend sacrifices for you and is not selfish towards you.
- A friend is an encouragement to you, not threatened by you.
- A friend treats you to things on occasion without expecting anything in return.
- A friend allows you to treat them to things on occasion without expecting anything in return.
- A friend does not indulge in self-destructive behaviors nor lead you down a similar path.

Did you learn anything interesting about yourself on your life's journey? What was it?

First of all, I agree that life is a journey. No matter where you are at any time, accomplishment or setback, there is still more ahead. There are 86,400 seconds in a day. Every day is a gift. We choose how we want to spend those seconds, those days, and as long as we have breath in our lungs the journey of life continues. I would say that the interesting thing that I've learned about myself is what I refer to as "self-awareness." Being self-aware means coming to an understanding of who you are, how you're wired, what you value. It means you are not confused about your purpose or value or why other people are some way and you are not. It's recognizing that there are things you just don't have any control over, so you don't allow these things to limit you. These could include who your parents are, the type of family you were raised in, the color of your skin, your height or weight (although everyone has some control over their weight). Being self-aware means you understand your personality type and you don't try to change it. By that I mean if you are an extrovert or introvert, academic or interactive, competitive or compliant. I know how God wired me, the things He has gifted me in and the things I just don't have in me. He has given me a love for meeting and being around people, teaching and mentoring youth, for talking about Christ, for writing, for loving my family, for wanting to do my part to leave a better world than the one I came into. He forgot to include a good singing voice for me, however.

What is the most important lesson you've learned about people?

I would say the most important thing I've learned about people is that everyone, I mean everyone, has problems. It doesn't matter if you are young, middle-aged, or old. Poor, middle class, or wealthy. Uneducated, educated, or scholar. European, Asian, Indian, or from the Americas. Everyone has problems. Certainly, some more than others. Life is filled with problems. Some are as the result of things done to us and others from things we've done to ourselves. These problems are not what God intended for us and for the world. Rather, it's a result of the decisions both we and others around us have made, some even from generations that came before us. What comes to mind is one of the movie clips that we use during CROP. It's the one where the dad is talking to his son about how nothing will hit you harder than life. But it's not about how hard you get hit, it's about getting back up and keep moving forward. Get back up and keep moving forward. That's how winning is done. So stop blaming things and people for your problems. This is the part where the lesson I've learned about people comes in. Since I know everyone has problems, I've learned to have more compassion for others. I give them the benefit of the doubt if something does not seem to be going well for them at the moment. I offer help if I can, humor when appropriate, and encouragement at all times. Most importantly, reminding them that Jesus is the ultimate helper, a friend in time of need. The One who enables us to do all things through Him. For those who have received Jesus as Lord and Savior, the day will come where all things have been restored as they were intended. No more sorrows. No more tears. No more struggle. No more pain. Only perfect peace, love, and joy, and the presence of the Father, Son, and Spirit.

Do you think life's fair? Tell me why it is or isn't.

In order to answer this question accurately, we have to agree on the definition of the word "fair." Unfortunately, that word, like many others, has had people use that to mean different things based on what they want it to mean. According to the dictionary, fair means "free from bias, dishonesty or injustice, free from self-interest, prejudice or favoritism." So, using that definition, then no, I don't think life is fair. Why? Because of what our culture favors, is self-indulgent in, and is partial in justice. In Western culture, favoritism falls towards the beautiful, youthful, physically fit, and wealthy. In other cultures, favoritism falls towards the older and wiser. Ethnically, some cultures have prejudice against Whites, Latinos, Asians, Blacks, or Indians. Injustices are imposed on different faith or belief systems, on political affiliation and socioeconomic class, and on levels of education. Bias and dishonesty are also expressed towards a person's biological sex, disability, or their physical features. However, there are two things that I think are important to know. First, all the unfairness in life is the result of attitudes and actions of mankind. With God, He shows partiality to no one. He loves all people perfectly and equally, and one day those who have called on the name of Jesus to be saved will experience that. Second, no matter what anyone's lot in life is, it's no excuse for self-pity or surrender. Numerous people in every walk of life have overcome great obstacles to fulfill their dreams and make a positive impact on others. Like I wrote earlier, no matter how fair or unfair you think life is, it's about getting back up and keeping on moving forward. Trusting in God in all things will help you to do that, even when you don't feel like doing it.

What golden rule do you want me to live by?

The golden rule I would like you to live by is THE Golden Rule: That is, treat others as you would like to be treated. Remember, the only things you have total 100% control over are your words and actions, nothing else. You have no control over what other people say to you or do to you, whether it be accidental or intentional. You have zero control over things that happen in your surroundings or in the world. All you have are your words and your actions. You can't even control your thoughts. So how would you like to be spoken to? Then speak that way to others. How would you like to be treated? Then treat others that way. It's as simple as that. Now for a couple of very important footnotes to this. First, you oftentimes don't know what is going on in someone's life right now. As I mentioned before, everyone has problems, some more than others. If this results in misbehavior towards you, give them the benefit of the doubt. Have some compassion and grace toward them, even when it means surrendering your right to retaliation. Second, and this one is very important, you need to protect yourself from harmful, evil people. That's right, there are people that will inflict harm on others by the things they say and by physical abuse (words and actions). Whatever their life's problems were or are, it doesn't mean you should tolerate this harm towards you. Sometimes these people are strangers. Sometimes they are neighbors, coworkers, friends, and even family. If they don't respond to your kindness, remove yourself from the situation.

> Everyone has problems, some more than others.

How did you know when you were in love?

Well, love is that thing that drives nearly all aspects of humankind. We all want someone to love, and we all want to be loved by someone. God designed us for love. We love because He loved us first. Whoever does not love does not know God, because God is love. Now it's important to understand that the English word "love" is so broad. I love my parents. I love my sister. I love my dog. I love pizza. I love football. Same word, but totally different sentiments, because that object of love is so different in each of these examples. In the context of this question, it's clear that it is referring to romantic love. In that light, romantic love really cannot begin until at least puberty begins. Part of romantic love entails physiological attraction to someone. It begins with noticing someone and thinking, "Ooh, I like what I see." It then moves to thinking about that person. A lot. You think of them more than of anyone else. You can't stop thinking of them. You fantasize about talking to them, spending time with them, and doing things with them. Eventually, actual communication takes place. You enjoy talking with each other, you choose to do things alone together, and eventually you touch each other. You hold hands, you hug, you kiss, and everything is fireworks. Your body tingles with emotion and you can't believe this person is feeling about you the way you feel about them. Eventually you want to commit your exclusive love toward that person, and you desire to give of yourself more than receive. Yes, true love is patient, kind, not envious or boastful, not proud, not self-seeking, not dishonorable, not angered. Love keeps no record of wrongdoing and does not delight in evil but rejoices in truth. Love always protects, trusts, hopes, and perseveres. Love never fails.

What is life's most precious commodity that shouldn't be wasted?

Time.

What should I do if I can't forgive someone?

Forgiveness is one of the most critical things in life that you must learn, with the discipline required to remain forgiving. The ability to forgive is a sign of maturity, and it doesn't come easy. I wrote a CROP lesson on the topic of forgiveness. What I wrote is that forgiveness means surrendering your right to retribution for a wrong that was done to you. Let's break that down. "Surrendering" means this is a decision of your will, it's your choice. Only you can choose whether or not to forgive. "Your right" means you're entitled to it. You deserve to dish out retribution. The "retribution" refers to payback. Dishing back harm for something that was done to you unjustly or unfairly. Remember, most people never feel like forgiving. Harm does hurt and hurt people tend to hurt people. But keep this in mind, and this part is very important. When you choose not to forgive, it doesn't hurt the other person nearly as much as it hurts you. Unforgiveness eats you up from the inside and tears apart your mind, emotions, and soul. Some people recognize the harm they have done and are genuinely repentant and ask forgiveness. Grant it to them and let it go. Don't bring it up again. Other people aren't aware of their harm or don't even care. Forgive them in your own heart and let it go. Be aware that forgiveness is not the same as tolerance. You should never have to, or be expected to, tolerate someone's ongoing harm toward you. Don't be fooled by anyone who consistently hurts you and then says they are sorry so that you will remain in their life. Do not put up with that, no matter who it is. You should separate yourself from that relationship until they can get help for themselves to stop that behavior. If or when you allow them back into your life, be cautious as they will have to earn back your trust over time.

What moments in your life do you relish the most?

So many great moments growing up, which changed as I got older:

Growing up: Playing with friends, going on vacation, going out to eat for my birthday, Christmas, Thanksgiving, Easter, 4th of July, watching TV, playing sports.

> Young adult years: Dating, driving places, meeting friends at clubs, dancing, running, traveling, vacations, and dating. Did I already mention dating? Good, I wanted to make sure you caught it the first time.
>
> Adult years: Meeting Jesus and learning about Him, worship, meeting your mom and dating, marrying her, seeing you when you were born, holding you in my arms, watching you sleep, reading stories to you at night, seeing you grow through different life stages, learning to be a parent, starting all over again when your sister was born, going on trips with your mom, spending time with family at gatherings.
>
> Currently: Going to bed, eating popcorn and watching TV with your mom, having a clean house and car, going out to eat, watching football with people, driving around Idaho, listening to music, golfing, reading God's word, anything related to CROP.

How's that for an exciting life!

Did you ever feel like giving up? What did you do? What should I do if I ever feel like giving up on something?

Yes, I've had plenty of times in my life that I felt like giving up. Everyone does. No matter what their level of success in all segments of humanity, we all feel like giving up. It's normal. When those times come, you will feel lost and like a total failure. Here are some examples in my life when I felt like giving up.

1. When my brother would beat me (in sports) and pick on me.
2. When I struggled to understand certain types of math.
3. When I was in a bad dating relationship.
4. When I was performing really poorly in sporting events.
5. When I struggled in and got fired from a job.
6. When I had extreme financial difficulties and couldn't provide for my family.
7. When I endured a major church division when I was on staff and on the elder board.
8. When I was tired of being a "good guy" Christian.
9. When I had no idea why God put me on this earth.
10. When I felt like CROP was going nowhere.

As you can see in these 10 examples, these were all seasons of my life that didn't last and that I eventually worked through. So here are the things that I did and that I would suggest for you.

1. Know "WHY" you are doing something. If it's for the right reason, keep on going, you'll work through it. If it's for the wrong reason, then quit. Some things are not worth pursuing.

2. Have friends that you can be honest with, who can encourage you to keep going.

3. Realize that perseverance produces character and character produces hope. Hope does not disappoint.

4. Know deep down in your soul that God is rooting for you. He never does things TO us, He only does things FOR us.

What is most valuable to you in this life?

No question, without doubt or hesitation, my relationship with Jesus Christ, God the Father, and Holy Spirit. Everything in this life will eventually fall away, even the very breath in my lungs. I don't focus on things that I can never keep. I only focus on that which I will never lose. That is, my relationship with God. Any one of us can spend so much time, talent and money on things that are temporary. They will never last. And most of the things we pursue are for our own pleasure, power, and possessions. Why? Why do we do this? One day we will lose all of it. We all came into this world through the womb of our mother and we all will return to the dust of the earth. So why place any value on anything in this life? There are only three things that will last for all eternity: God, His Word, and the souls of mankind. Because of my conviction in that, my greatest contribution I can value is my relationship with God, while also doing whatever I can to ensure I help to connect the souls of people to God for all eternity, rather than seeing them separated from Him. That is why CROP is so important to me. Through CROP, I have the opportunity to bring teens and their parents onto the eternal path of Christ, if they're not already on it, and to keep them there if they are. I have a chance to use what God has woven into me in order to contend for the souls of men and women, and possibly play a part in their eternal salvation. Can you think of anything in life more valuable than that? I can't.

Tell me about a crossroads in your life and what you did. How did you make a decision about what to do?

There were several ones in my life. I'll list a few:

1. When I went to work with my dad when I was young, and I decided I wanted to go into business just like he was. He told me I should go to college to have the best chance at business, and I did.

2. I was going to go directly into university out of high school, but I was offered a scholarship to compete in track and field at community college. I would have never made a university team, so I went to community college and ran there. I'm really glad I did.

3. In my search for spiritual truth and meaning, I discovered that the Bible was the source of truth, and THAT truth was Jesus Christ. This happened on Thursday, February 26, 1987, at 1:13 PM.

4. About six months after that day, I was faced with a decision to marry my girlfriend of two years, who was not a believer and had refused to believe in Christ, or to be obedient and choose to be equally yoked with a Christian woman. I chose obedience to Christ, which to this day was the hardest decision I've ever made. But Jan, your mom, has been my reward for obedience.

5. In 2002, I left my business career of 16 years to go into full-time ministry. This decision came on the heels of a lot of prayer. Despite the really hard time that I went through, I truly believe God had me there for the reason I served.

How does the idea of becoming a grandparent make you feel?

Well, as you know, I already AM one! Here's the story. I always say that I "suffer" from young man mind and old man memory. While the "memory" part is easy to understand (I forget a lot of things), my mind often thinks, acts, and says things like a young man. I often think of things the same way I did when I was in my 20s, although I'm much calmer and wiser now. So the idea of becoming a grandparent made me feel old. I've never felt very old at all. I still don't. I know I joke about it all the time, but I don't think I look or feel very old. Certainly not my actual age. I attribute that to my consistent exercise, fairly good nutrition, and my genetics. When you were pregnant with Anthony, Mom got more and more excited as your delivery date drew near. She would often ask me, "Are you getting excited yet?" to which I'd reply, "Nope." It's not that I was angry, upset, or had any negative feelings or attitudes about your pregnancy. Rather, my mindset was that I should FIRST look and feel old before I should be a grandpa. I felt that way even at the hospital.

And then he was born!

Oh my gosh, it all changed in an instant!! I took one look at that sweet baby boy, and I was immediately in love. He was perfect! And I still think he is. My feelings of being a grandpa literally changed in an instant when I took one look at Anthony. My joy of being a grandparent increased even more when your second son, Cayden was born. So yes, the idea of being a grandparent is way super cool!

Did you ever want to travel the world? If you could go anywhere you wanted, where would you go and why?

Well, actually, I have traveled the world (kind of). So far, I have traveled to 46 of the 50 States and have been to 13 countries. When I was 17 years old, my family took a five-week trip to Europe. We visited seven countries on that trip. I really enjoyed it a lot and I'm so thankful we went. Why? It wasn't as much for the sightseeing. Rather, it was for my takeaway from that trip. I had always looked at the United States as the best place on earth, and that the rest of the world was jealous of us because they weren't Americans. But what I observed in each of those countries is that all the people were just like us. They wanted the same things that we want. They want someone to love and someone to be loved by. They wanted families. They wanted a job that they could work hard in and be able to provide for themselves. They wanted to play sports, watch sports, appreciate art, and enjoy entertainment. They wanted a warm home to live in, good food to eat, and great wine and beer. They wanted to be able to rest and they wanted freedom. That experience recalibrated my attitude on what I thought of America and how I valued people. Only two years later, I had an opportunity to see my own country when three friends of mine and I traveled the country in a Volkswagen bus. We drove through 35 states, two provinces of Canada, a total of 10,200 miles in 5 1/2 weeks. It was awesome! I was truly amazed at how many different cultures there are in our own nation. A wonderful variety and no such thing as a "typical" American. The one place I have not yet been to, that I would really like to see someday, is the Holy Land of Israel. To walk the path of Jesus and experience His portion of the world would be beyond words for me.

How did you handle betrayal in your life?

I really had to think hard on this one. I struggled with coming up with any betrayal experiences. The one and only one that I could consider a betrayal event was when we went through the church split. You were too young, so you may not remember it. At the time I was on the elder board of the church, and I was on full-time staff. I had reached a point in my life where the more that I served and ministered to people, the more I felt God's pleasure. I wanted more of it, and I was in a position where I was receiving it. What I didn't know when I joined the elder board and the staff, was that there was a small but influential group of people that were discontented with certain aspects, decisions, and leadership of the church. They allowed this bitter root to set in their discontentment, and that bitter root grew. They secretly started spreading sordid stories and having private meetings to scheme against the leadership of the church. What started as 26 discontent families grew to 80 in a church that had 904 households on our roster. Some of the families that were seduced into this tribe were friends of mine. I suddenly saw looks of anger, despise, and disgust in their eyes towards me and towards Mom. She in no way deserved that. It's one thing when a friend betrays you, but it's even worse when you add the spiritual element of church family. Thankfully, some of those relationships have been mended, while others never will be. Review my writing on "forgiveness" 7 pages prior.

What rule did your parents teach you that turned out to be the most important rule of all?

I'm not sure if there was any particular rule per se that they intentionally taught or impressed upon me. Several principles were taught in our home that I had previously written about. Things like treating others as you would like to be treated, valuing education, hard work, value people, take responsibility, and own your mistakes. But when I was thinking about this question, the one thing that kept coming back to mind was the importance of family. I'm not sure they ever taught that as a lesson. Rather, they lived it as a lesson. So much of what we did when I was growing up was together, not in isolation. We ate meals together, went on numerous vacations together. We did things for each other. Home was always the place that we wanted to come back to, where we would invite friends, families, and even strangers to. I've always felt family was an important entity to work on, invest in, and value. It's based on the foundation of love and is demonstrated not in selfishness but sacrifice. When unplanned things happen in life, everyone should rally around and help each other out. That's what families should do. I'm aware, and probably you are too, that all families do not function that way. Probably most do not. They grew up or live in brokenness, which breaks my own heart. That is not what God ever intended. But that is something only God can heal. He gives us the opportunity to be adopted into a spiritual family, a functional one.

Has anything from your past haunted you? What was it?

Again, I'm not really recalling anything major that I would consider a past haunting. No deep, dark secrets. No skeletons in the closet. However, one incident has always come back to mind, and I just can't shake the memory. It may sound really dumb, really minor, and when I share it, you may say, "Really? That's it?" Or you may say, "Yeah, I get it." So here it is. When I was in high school, I was a member of a community service club. Many of our members would hang out separately from club activities and we became friends. One time after a club activity, several of us decided impromptu to get together later that evening and do something fun. I don't recall what it was, but it was something you wanted to be at. We decided we would all go home to ask our parents if it was OK to go and then we would meet up. There was a sweet, really nice girl in the group to whom I said, "You should go with us. It will be a lot of fun. Ask your parents if you can go and I'll come and pick you up. I'll call you." She said OK. So our group met up, we went to the place, and we had a great time. Later that week at school, I saw her. I asked her why she wasn't there. She said, "You never called." Wow, I didn't. I'll never forget that look on her face or the sound in her voice. "You never called." I didn't. What played in my mind, what plays in my mind, what "haunts" me is what probably played out in her house. She shares her excitement of being invited, being included in the fellow teen activity. She convinces her mom to let her go, knowing how important it is to be included as a teen. The girl puts on one of her favorite outfits and waits in excited anticipation for a great night out. But I never called.

In what ways do you feel blessed?

I feel blessed in almost every way imaginable. First, that I hit a point in my life as a young adult where I knew something was missing in my life. Although I had pretty much everything that a 26-year-old could want, there was a deep void within my soul that caused me to search for spiritual truth and meaning. I discovered that what I was missing was Jesus. I was missing His forgiveness, His love, and His clarity for my life. I also feel blessed with the family I was born into, the home I was raised in and the upbringing I had. I feel blessed with the wife that I married, the children we adopted, and the grandchildren I have. I'm blessed with my health. To be at my age and not have any injuries, ailments, or disabilities is something I'm truly grateful for. Being able to exercise like I do and to really enjoy foods that are good for me is a really great thing. I feel blessed with the personality I have, the gifts that God has given me, the things that I enjoy. I feel especially blessed that I discovered the reason that God put me on this earth. It seems to me that most people go through life never knowing the meaning of life or why they are here on this earth. I believe one of the highest obligations in life is to know why you were born, and the highest obligation is living your life for God's purpose.

Did you ever experience a miracle? If so, what?

The term "miracle" and its application to life events is one of those words with a somewhat broad definition, along with a loose application of the word, depending on who is using it. One definition pertains to an event or effect that deviates from the laws of nature. Another definition refers to a supernatural act of a divine agent (that is, God or a deity). A third definition refers to a wonder or a wonderful thing. I'm not sure that I ever personally experienced a miracle which defied the laws of nature, science, or medicine. But I have several friends who have. However, I do believe in a couple of miracles that I say were as the result of a divine agent (God), which was also an event that was filled with wonder (wonderful). Those would be the circumstances which brought you into this world to become our daughter, and the circumstances that brought Anthony into this world to become your son. God was all over those two stories, and nobody can convince me otherwise.

What are you most thankful for in your life today?

I know this is starting to sound redundant, but clearly the most thankful thing in my life today is my personal relationship with God the Father and Holy Spirit through Jesus the Son. Everything in my life is not only a byproduct of this, but it's also what makes every aspect of my life complete, fulfilling, and understandable. Without an understanding of God, it is impossible to understand life, its meaning, and our purpose for it. Life is an absolute gift. There is so much joy and excitement that it offers. Jesus said that He came to earth so that we might have life and that it would be abundant (fulfilling) - John 10:10. What a tragedy to live a wasted life! A life devoid of meaning, purpose, and fulfillment. When people live a life without Jesus, there is a hole, a void that can only be filled with Him. They look for a substitute to fill that emptiness in their heart and soul. They often look to false substitutes that typically turn into addictions. These could include smoking, drugs, alcohol, pornography, sex, money, possessions, power, greed, anger, and all sorts of vices that never lead to any good. We were created in God's image, and only when we know Him can we see His reflection in us when we look inward and examine ourselves. You only need to look at the high and increasing rates of addictions, depression, suicide, homelessness, broken families, and false religions to validate that truth.

Tell me what you know about the phrase "nothing lasts forever" and "you don't know what you've got until it's gone."

Remember what I wrote about earlier? We're all born into this world with nothing (naked), and we will leave with nothing. It is impossible to take anything from this world into the next (that is, being with God, or being separated from Him for all eternity). So as a result, nothing ever lasts forever except the souls of mankind. In that dash that will appear on our gravestones, which separates the year we were born and the year we die, lies all the things we did, experienced, and accumulated on this earth. Some of those things will have been necessities such as food, clothing, and knowledge. Other things include homes, cars, possessions, and relationships. We tend to take many things for granted and don't really value them until they are gone. For example, our health. Everything about our health we often take for granted. But how would your life be different if you lost your ability to see, hear, speak, smell, or feel? What if you couldn't walk, digest food, or maintain your balance? How would life be different if you had no clothes to wear, no bed to sleep in, or no home to live in? What will life be like when the day comes that you lose a parent, sibling, spouse, close friend, or God forbid, a child? These are all things that we often take for granted. We don't "know what we had until it is gone." None of the things I mentioned will last forever, except the souls, the spirits of the people who accepted Jesus Christ as their Savior. They, with us, will one day be raised into a new body that will dwell with God in the heavenly places for all eternity. Hallelujah!

Dad, is honesty always the best policy?

Yes, honesty is always the best policy. However, please understand that a policy is a guideline, rules in which to operate by. A policy attempts to establish best practices in the environment it's intended for, but it doesn't have to be an absolute. There can be exceptions. There are several advantages to living a life of honesty. First, you don't have to remember a lie that you may have told. It's always easy to remember the truth because the truth is actually what happened. It's just a matter of recalling the event that happened and then retelling it. If an event is clothed in a lie or in dishonesty, you have to remember what you said, which isn't easy. Second, honesty is a reflection of your character. People will trust and respect you if you're honest with them. They won't if you're not. Third, honesty helps to convict others when they are dishonest. While this is not always the case, most people will be dishonest to you if you are dishonest with them. So when is it acceptable to be dishonest with someone, to lie to them? I would say if you were in imminent danger. If physical harm may come around you, I think it's OK to be dishonest. An example is if someone who seems sketchy to you tries to engage you in conversation or wants to come into the house when you are alone, it would be OK to say, "Wait here, let me go get my husband." Close the door and lock it. Now keep in mind that if you may get in trouble because of something you were negligent in, then it's not OK to be dishonest just to get out of trouble. Take responsibility, take your medicine, and own your mistake. People will respect you more than if you try to cast blame elsewhere.

What bad trait do you have that always got you into trouble? Do I have it too?

I can't think of anything that always got me into trouble, but one thing that comes to mind is that I used to interrupt people in order to speak what was on my mind. I still do it on occasion, but I am more aware of it now and I try to catch myself when I do it. I don't think you really do that, but your mom does! (I hope she doesn't read this...)

What should I never waste energy on?

Placing value on the opinions of people that don't matter. This doesn't mean that you don't value advice and direction from people that love you and that you trust. Becoming a better person should be a lifelong pursuit. Everyone can always become more loving, more generous, more kind. What I'm talking about here is people who are critical, mean, condescending, destructive. Some people in life are so wounded that they only know how to wound others. They haven't learned to forgive others or themselves. They also don't know what it means to be forgiven. They go through life trying to tell you what you are, what you should be. They make you feel like you are deficient, incomplete, and insufficient. Don't waste your time, energy, or concern on them.

What's one of the hardest things we will have to do in life?

Learn discipline. Being disciplined in so many areas of our lives is oftentimes the hardest thing for us to do. Why? Because being undisciplined is easy. It's comfortable. It's pleasurable. But discipline is hard. Yet what does it do? It builds strength. It builds character. It builds confidence. It builds peace. It builds resistance to temptations that can lead us down a wrong path towards self-destructive behaviors. Discipline means doing the right things even when you don't feel like it because they are good for you. What are some things that require discipline? Exercise, what you eat, going to work, praying, reading your Bible, saving money, controlling anger, patience, managing your sexuality, forgiving, showing acts of love, not wasting time. Using the gifts that God has given you.

What have you learned about trusting people?

I always bestow trust to everyone up front. That is, I assume that each person is trustworthy until or unless they prove themselves to be untrustworthy. I think most people have been hurt or betrayed by someone else. A man, woman, friend, coach, pastor, church member, family member, employer. You name it. Just because one or more members of a particular group betrayed your trust, it doesn't mean they all will. It's important and fair to evaluate each person's character individually. Now, if that person betrays your trust, does that mean you never trust them again? Not necessarily. You'll need to evaluate if that offense was a one-off or is it habitual. If a one-off, then forgive, but watch. If habitual, then limit your exposure to that person. They don't deserve you.

What's your biggest regret in life?

I've had to think long and hard about how to answer this one. I read it over and over again and have had about three weeks pass since my last journal entry trying to figure out how to answer. My initial thoughts were that I couldn't think of any life regrets. Sure, there have been disappointments, setbacks, and hardships. I've made some poor decisions and there are some do-overs that I can think of which would be nice. However, I really had trouble thinking of anything that I would consider my "biggest" regret. Until now.

I mentioned this earlier with another question, so I'll reiterate it here. What comes to mind as my biggest regret is my unwillingness to learn and apply principles of money management. As I reflect back on my life and my career, I would say I've earned a lot of money. But due to my negligence and inattention, I've also spent a lot. Should I say I've wasted a lot? I've done a poor job at living the principle of spending less than you make. While money is not the most important thing in life, it certainly is a huge one. Everything in life and anything you do (mostly) requires money. While God is our provider and He promises that He knows our daily needs, it's still our responsibility to do our part and exercise good judgment on money matters. Learn and apply this principle now, and you'll be glad you did when you get to be my age.

— Chapter 5 —
GROWING OLDER

What do you wish someone had told you about life when you were younger?

Actively seek out mentors throughout your life, learn to apply their wisdom, and filter out what doesn't apply to you. And don't be afraid to ask for help. I've learned that wise, successful people typically have endured hardships and disappointments along their journey. Yet through perseverance, they eventually overcome these obstacles and they developed systems and habits in their lives which contributed to their success. Just about everything in life is hard. Things that come easily typically don't last or they are not worth it. Everything in life that we see or know was done by someone. Somebody did what was required to dream, build, create, produce, accomplish. I'm certain that none of it came easy, despite them sometimes making it look easy. The countless amounts of hours and efforts are typically not seen or measured by others. Some things we only get one shot at, and we never have another chance. No matter what it is that God puts on your heart, just go for it. Expect that there will most likely be disappointments and setbacks along the way. It's possible you may never even accomplish "that thing." Just do your best. Don't leave any room for regrets where you know you could have done better, and don't let that thing define you in success or failure. What you do is never who you are.

Does life get easier as you grow older?

In many areas, yes. As you get older, wiser, and more mature, things don't typically affect you in the same way. Emotions don't run as high, there's not as much drama, and you kind of learn that no matter how bad things may seem, you realize that everything is going to be OK. I remember when Anthony was born. He was only two days old, and I was sharing with someone that I am now a grandpa and how it seemed so amazingly wonderful to be a grandpa the very moment he was born. I'll never forget what that person said. "You know, Mark, I think being a grandparent is almost better than being a parent. Don't get me wrong. I love my kids just as much as I know that you love yours. But when you're a parent, you're pretty much just trying to figure it all out. What to do. How to do it. School, friends, sports, discipline. You're never sure if you're doing it right. You certainly don't want to do anything that might screw up their lives. But when you're a grandparent, you're typically calmer, wiser, more financially secure. In fact, I think my hopes and dreams for my grandchildren are greater than they ever were for my own kids." I thought about that for a moment and then I said, "Oh my gosh, I think you're right!" I think the one thing that does not get easier when you get older is your health. It's so important to establish healthy lifestyle habits now while you're young so that it's not so hard to maintain them when you are older.

> **Establish healthy lifestyle habits now.**

Looking back, what do you wish you'd made more time for?

Creating more memories with you. Both memories with just us and memories as a family. When you girls were growing up, we really struggled financially. I take ownership of that because there were things I could have done differently to put us in a better position. I regret that we did not take more vacations and introduce you to more places. Living in Southern California, there were so many places to see and visit that didn't even cost that much. But it requires planning and being intentional to carve out those moments. I wish I would have done more. I'm so sorry.

What is your proudest life accomplishment thus far?

Keeping my family intact. I've seen so many damaged families, so many ruined lives. I've seen failed marriages and blood relatives so embittered with one another. It's so tragic to see. Yet here we are. As of this writing, Mom and I have been married for 30 1/2 years. I've never cheated on her, and I know she has never cheated on me. Despite challenges, hardships, and disagreements, we always wanted to work things out. We never, ever got close to a divorce discussion. That just wasn't an option for us. I have seen so many families that are damaged as a result of divorce. I think that keeping our marriage together has had a huge impact on keeping our overall family together. I recall the tremendous difficulties I had with your sister during her teen years and how things could have really gone the wrong way if I said or did any of the things I felt. I think of your unplanned pregnancy and how different things could be if we had responded differently and you had made another choice. Life is so filled with challenges, struggles and things unplanned. Yet love conquers all. Just as the Apostle Paul wrote so eloquently in 1 Corinthians 13, love never fails. I'm thankful and proud that I honestly think I did my best in showing and living love within our family and I think it has worked.

What is your favorite memory about fatherhood in general?

The day you were born. The day your sister was born. The day I became a grandpa. All of those are such huge milestones in life. And they change you forever. You are filled with such a sense of awe and excitement, not knowing what the future is going to hold. At the same time, you are infused with this huge sense of responsibility on "how am I going to do this?" You learn to take each moment at a time. I clearly remember being very aware that the time with you girls was going to go by so quickly, so I wanted to be fully present whenever we had special moments together. That includes when we would read books together, when I would lay down with you at bedtime to tell you stories, and I would usually fall asleep before you did. I love the times that I would be walking with you girls, and we would be holding hands, or I'd be carrying you on my shoulders. I loved the times when we would arrive home at night after being away for a while and you girls fell asleep in your car seat. I would get you out while you were still asleep, and I'd carry you up to your bed as your sleepy head would rest on my chest and shoulder. Those were some of the most precious memories I've ever had, and I'm so thankful that I was allowed to have them.

What are you currently looking forward to in your life right now?

I'm looking forward to taking CROP nationwide and eventually worldwide so that I can have the opportunity to impact families and generations to come. I am crystal clear on how God has wired me, how He has equipped me, and what He has called me to do. I'm so excited, and yet so afraid to fulfill the mission He has given me. I realized that so many families do not have the tools to effectively raise the next generation, and I believe CROP will be a resource for them. I fully believe that if I am faithful to complete what God has tasked me with, then He will be faithful to provide for Mom and me. As I wrote earlier, our financial future is far from secure. That is why Mom and I continue to work. But we can't continue to work at this pace forever. I can see the toll that it is taking on Mom. If, by God's favor, He decides to use CROP as the vehicle to provide for our financial future, then so be it. I know the promises, that God knows our daily needs and He will provide for them. How He does it is up to Him.

How much sacrifice did you have to make in life? In what ways and was the reward worth the sacrifice?

I'm really struggling with this question and how to accurately answer it. When I think of the word "sacrifice," what I think of is the deliberate act of forsaking something you want now to obtain something better for yourself or someone else later. On one hand, I recall hearing stories of world-champion athletes who never had friends, went to parties, went on dates, had a boyfriend/girlfriend growing up, due to the demands of their training. Their reward? Victory in their sport. And on the other hand, I think of the parents that worked two or three jobs to make enough money so that their kid can go to school. Their reward? A child who has the ability to accomplish more and live a better life than the parent did. When I consider these two examples, I don't see myself in either of them. I feel that for most of my life I've been somewhat selfish. I mostly did what I wanted to do and bought what I wanted to buy. When times were financially tough, I never humbled myself to take an hourly job or switch careers to take a steady paying job. I pursued the things that I wanted to do so that I could have the freedom and flexibility in my schedule to do what I wanted to do. I probably could have done a much better job at truly sacrificing in order to have obtained a better reward. I would say the biggest lesson I learned that I would now like to pass on to you, is this: there is a difference between what you want to do and what you _need_ to do. When the two are in alignment, then great. When not, you have to be honest with yourself and place a higher priority on what you _need_ to do. That is true sacrifice, and that is probably where the rewards will come from.

> There is a difference between what you want to do and what you need to do.

Did you ever think you'd end up where you are now in life?

In most ways, yes. I always knew I would get married and that my intent was that it was for life. I never wanted to have to go through a divorce. I envisioned my marriage would be a fulfilling marriage in which my wife and I would be happy. And here we are, married 30 1/2 years as I write this, and I feel it is all that. I wanted children, a minimum of two and ideally three or four, and here I have you and your sister. Of course, we didn't expect that we'd have to go the route of adoption in order to have children due to our infertility. But that part has turned out way better than I ever imagined. I never looked at you or your sister as anything other than my/our children, and I've never once to this day ever yearned for a biological child of my own. I always thought I would end up in a comfortable middle-class lifestyle, which we have. I felt that family unity would be one of the pillars of strength in my life, and I feel I have that on my side of the family, on my mom's side, and even on your biological birth family side. When I came to faith in Christ at age 26, I expected I would stay true to those beliefs and never wander from the faith, to which I have remained faithful. The only area that I fell short of is in the area of finances. I thought we would be in a better position. But God has been our provider, and He will see us through.

If you could have met anyone famous at any point in your life, who would it have been and why?

I've met a small handful of famous people in my life, people wherein I shook their hand and had a personal one-on-one conversation with, even if for only a moment. The first one to come to mind is Ronald Reagan. He was an actor, former governor of California, and became a two-term President of the United States. My parents were very involved in politics when I was growing up, so it was very special to meet him. Next is Tom Scholz, founder of the rock group Boston. I loved their music when I was a teen and I still do. I met him in a hotel lobby in Chicago when I was traveling on business. In high school and college, I ran track and field, and I love watching it to this day. A prominent personality is Dwight Stones. He was a world-class high jumper and an Olympic athlete. He became a national broadcaster of track and field events. I met him outside a movie theater in Foothill Ranch. Regarding any other famous people that I haven't met, I guess I would include Farrah Fawcett and Cheryl Tiegs, fashion models when I was a teenager because I was a teenager. Musician Neil Diamond, because I love his music. Mary Decker Slaney, world class track athlete, because of her drive and commitment to win.

Where did you always want to live that you never got the chance?

Nothing comes to mind about this one. Being born and raised in California, I came to believe that it was the best place in the world to live. People from across the nation and around the world either came to live there or wanted to. By the time I was in my early 30s, I had traveled to 46 of the 50 States and 13 different countries. I saw a lot of beautiful land and culture, yet I would still say, "There's no place like home." I never longed to live any place else. But I have changed, and so has California. It no longer holds the same place in my heart. I'm very happy with where I currently live. I feel the values of this local culture align best with Mom's and my values. There is no place else that I am aware of at this time that I would rather live, nor has there been any other place in the past that drew me without my responding.

What should I never forget to do?

Love your mother and hug your dad.

Who or what was your best teacher about life?

My best teacher about life has been LIFE. I know that sounds like circular reasoning, but so much that there is to learn about life cannot be taught in a classroom. I learned early on to observe other people, see what went into their decision making and how those decisions turned out. Fortunately for me, I saw a lot of people doing a lot of stupid things and it turned out badly for them. I would conclude, "Well, that was dumb. I'm not going to do that!" It saved me from lots of pain and setbacks in my life. So who are the great teachers in life about LIFE? I would say Observation. Watching what others did and seeing how that turned out. I would include Wisdom and Logic. What makes sense, and could I expect a similar outcome if I did the same or the opposite? I will also add Risk and Adventure. There has to be a certain level of thrill and adventure to be willing to try something that you may not have done before and being willing to risk failure. Don't forget Mentors. They are great life teachers as well. They love to pour into others their own knowledge and experience, and they want to help others be successful.

What is one thing that didn't turn out the way you'd hoped, and how did you wish it had turned out?

I had to think about this one for a long time. I read the question, and I didn't come back to it for several days as I pondered my response. What finally came to mind was this: my level of success. That is, the level of success that I reached in a few areas of my life. I wish it would have been much greater than it has been. Granted, I am very happy about how my marriage turned out. I'm happy with how we became a family through your adoption and how Anthony and Cayden became part of our family. I'm happy with both my side and Mom's side of the family, as well as how we have been forever knit together with your birthmother Sunni's family. I'm happy with our home, where we live, our cars, possessions, etc. What I feel did not turn out the way I hoped was my level of success in sports (high school and college), career, and finances. I feel I have the talent and capabilities to have accomplished more than I did. I think if I was more focused, more determined, more disciplined, and stuck with things longer, then I would have had more success. Fortunately, none of these areas where I feel I came up short are things that haunt me or that I have deep regrets about. They are (were) not more important than the family things I mentioned earlier. I would much rather take my great family and moderate success than a moderate family with great success.

What problems of the world today trouble you?

World politics. The acceleration of world leaders is rapidly moving the world population to a one-world government. What does this all mean? There will no longer be any place or nation on earth that will be sovereign, that will be independent and a place of refuge. All people of the world will be required to comply with the government rule or else. They will either be cut off (cancelled) from all society (no work, no shopping, no money, no home to live in), or they will be exterminated. That's right. Their life will be taken from them, either through execution or starvation or exposure to disease. These government world leaders will be tyrants. There will be no rights of individuals. The masses of the people will be a threat to these leaders, so these leaders will manipulate and bully the masses into compliance. All of this should be no surprise to us though. The world got a good taste of this via the COVID-19 "pandemic" that we all suffered through in 2020 – 2022. This was all foretold by the writers of the Bible and by Jesus Himself over 2000 years ago. And here we are. We are seeing all this play out right before our eyes. My heart absolutely breaks for you and our grandchildren. However, I'm comforted in the fact that both you and I know the only way out, the only salvation of what's to come. That is Jesus. He is our rock, our firm foundation, and our only hope.

Did you ever experience unrequited love?

Yes, I did. Only once in my life. But I remember. I had recently become a Christian and I had broken up with my girlfriend of 2 1/2 years due to incompatibility in faith. As I've alluded to in my earlier writings, I've always desired female companionship from the age of 14. My values had completely changed, so now my attention was out for someone who shared the same faith and values. There was a very cute, sweet girl that was in our young adults' group. I don't remember her name. We started hanging out together a lot. We went on hikes, bike rides, movies, ate out, cooked meals at home. For any two single adults that hung out as much as we did, they would have been considered dating. But we weren't. I wanted to. Badly. But she just wasn't interested. She was fine just being friends. Every time I tried to move the needle just a bit to transition beyond friendship, she would gently rebuff the move. No hand holding, no hugs, no kisses. I remember telling my roommate at the time that I literally felt a physical pain in my heart and chest because I desired a dating relationship with her. But I couldn't have it. I'm not certain how that all ended, but I'm pretty sure she moved back to another state where she had moved from and where all her family lived. P.S. great news, I don't have an ounce of longing or feeling for her anymore, because your mom completes me!

Does wisdom come from age?

No. I've known older people that were stupid and younger people that were wise. I think wisdom comes from experience, awareness, and education. With experience I'm referring to life experience. Things that you have gone through personally which gives you insights that you would never have had if it wasn't for that. Oftentimes the greatest life experience teachers are your failures. Whether decisions you made, things you said, something you tried, where your takeaway was, "Well, that didn't work." Of course, positive and successful life experiences can also be teachers of wisdom. However, one thing that I've learned (wisdom), is that failures are my greatest teachers. Which leads to awareness. If you're not aware of how things that happen around you, along with the decisions you make, affect the outcomes, then you'll never become wiser.

> **Wisdom comes from life experience, awareness, and education.**

You'll continue to make those same mistakes over and over again. Awareness means you take in the information, and you learn from it to help make your life better. The learning part leads to a third element, which is education. I'm not necessarily referring to classroom education like in high school or college. It could include that. But I'm mostly referring to self-education, where you read books and articles, attend seminars and workshops, listen to podcasts and blogs, and sign up for classes that pertain to things that interest you. Things that you want to learn in order to gain wisdom for you in areas that are important to you. Life experience, awareness, and education. That's where wisdom comes from, not just age.

What was the one thing you always tried to shelter your child/children from?

Predators. I'm not talking about the fictional predators in the movie series. Rather people who want to take something from you and would harm you in the process. There are so many types of predators that lurk in this evil world. The first is the child sex predator. These are deranged people with damaged, sex-addicted minds. They are either hooked on child pornography, child sex, or both. They got that way because they chose not to exercise any self-control in the lusts of their flesh. They know what they do is wrong, which is why they always operate in secret. Other predators are rapists. In a similar way, their brains are damaged as a result of their choices, and they actually enjoy taking sex by force from someone unwilling, and they usually like to hurt them in the process. Other predators are drug dealers. They get people hooked on drugs so that they can profit off of them. When they get people to the point where they can no longer afford the drug but are so addicted, they will do anything for them. The dealer then turns them into a drug runner, a drug dealer, or a prostitute. I would say that predators would also include bullies. They constantly look for weaker people to pick on to make them feel better about themselves. Finally, I always tried to shelter you from things that were not intended for children. That includes profane and hurtful language, violence, use of tobacco and alcohol and tattoos. Yes, I know you always wanted tats since you were young. That's why I always told you no until you turned 18, at which point you can decide for yourself. Although I'm certain there are experiences you had before you turned 18 that I don't know about, I hope I did a good job sheltering you.

What are your plans for retirement?

Well, I wish I could say that I have these lavish plans for retirement. Our Western culture encourages us to retire, take it easy, travel the world, pick up a hobby, and transition from being a producer to a consumer. In other words, stop providing value to others in exchange for money and simply start spending your retirement money for your personal pleasure. While many times that idea seems attractive, I don't think I could ever accept that idea of retirement. Certainly, the initial reason why is that I just did not put away enough money yet to allow that lifestyle. But I think the main reason why I don't think I could ever do that is because I don't want to waste all that God has invested in me. I'm keenly aware of the life experiences, awareness, and education He has given me (i.e., wisdom). I know where my heart, passion, and talents lie. To stop using all of that just so that I could rest and indulge myself in recreation seems so pointless to me. I would rather spend what some would call "retirement years" doing things focused on teaching and mentoring others. I see myself developing different Christian Rites of Passage (CROP) programs for different life stages. These would become the markers which people would look forward to as they transition from one life stage to another.

In what ways are you still like a child?

Ha! Where do I begin? Certainly, in the way I joke around. You know me. I'm always coming up with funny statements, making people laugh. I often say things that may not sound very adult-ish. I goof around a lot. I don't take a lot of things too seriously. You've heard me say, "I suffer from young man mind and old man memory." My thoughts are often very similar to when I was a young man, some of which would probably not be considered very mature. At times I will look upon men my age, even younger, and see a person who appears to be very stoic, very composed, proper, and dignified. For a short moment I will think to myself, "Why can't I be more like him?" Then I say, "Nah, that would be boring." I believe that one of the things that can really help us be content in life is to be ourselves, who we are naturally. Don't try to be somebody else just because you think you should. Rather, be who God created you to be. He gave you the personality you have because He loves variety. Now, to be clear, this does not mean you have freedom to be irresponsible or to engage in sinful behavior. I think we all have some of those desires in us. Rather, enjoy and rejoice in your uniqueness. Strive to grow intellectually, emotionally, and spiritually. Do your part to make your world better. Refrain from doing wasteful or sinful things. Don't compare yourself to others and be thankful for who you are.

What can you never be too careful about?

Several things come to mind. First, you can never be too careful about saving money. As I earlier wrote, I've done a terrible job at this and now Mom and I are making up for it. You can never be too careful about taking care of your body. This includes protecting yourself from injury as much as possible. Exercise. Be careful what you eat. Moderate alcohol consumption if you choose to drink. Don't smoke, vape, or take illegal drugs. If your body's not doing well, it affects every other area of your life. You can never be too careful about your surroundings when you are in public. Be aware of people around you, the environment you are in, where you sit, what you see. When driving, what are other drivers doing on all four sides of your car? You can never be too careful about protecting your kids from predators, bullies, online media, and their own self-destructive behaviors. You can never be too careful about figuring out when people are lying to you. Liars often use deception and seductive words to make their points seem plausible, when in fact they are untrue. We see a lot of that in our current culture, especially our current political leaders. They say and do so many selfish and harmful things, and they make it sound good for all. Do not be deceived. Wrong is always wrong, no matter how it is packaged. You'll need to learn how to spot untruths and stand against them whenever you can. Listen to people who have proven themselves to be faithful and true and disregard those who are not.

What lessons did you learn about money that you want me to know?

- It's impossible to save too much.
- It's possible to save too little.
- It's hard to learn and practice the discipline of saving.
- Everything will cost way more the older you get.
- Always be thinking of ways to generate multiple streams of income.
- Don't be afraid of investing time and money in a venture that can make you more money if you really want to do it and will commit.
- Never sign up for someone's "business opportunity" right away. Thank them very much. Go away and think about/pray on it for two weeks and then if you really want to do it for you, not them, then go for it.
- When you start a business venture, don't expect your friends to become your customers, but you can expect your customers to become friends.

What makes you laugh now, that made you furious back then?

Little kids. When I was younger (teen years), I could not stand little kids. They were loud, messy, demanding, and just plain annoying. I felt that they were so self-centered, which I really despised about them. Then one day, I realized, so was I. I didn't realize that when I looked at the behavior of little kids, I was really looking into a mirror, and I didn't like what I was seeing. I started changing my attitude and my behavior to become less self-centered and to be more giving. The more I changed, the more I started liking little kids. Nowadays, I really enjoy kids. I love to make them laugh and I delight in trying to teach them something.

What is the one thing you want people (family, friends, etc.) to remember most about you?

I've actually thought about this, probably more so than others. I have a picture in my mind of what the response would be when news breaks that I have died, and then what my funeral would look like. I envision that not only family and friends would be mourning my loss, but thousands of other people that I may or may not have ever met but were impacted by CROP or some other writings that I've published. My hope and prayer are that the materials I produce will have had an impact on numerous people across the country and around the world. That lives will have been changed for the better, and people will have been drawn closer to God in the process. At the same time, I hope to have conveyed along the way that human life in this world is only temporary for every one of us. Our eternal spiritual existence is what is most important. I hope that as time goes on, family and friends would recall good and funny memories of our time together. That they would be glad that I was a part of their life and that there would be some positive aspects of my life which they would integrate into their own. I would hope that family would say, "Well-lived life, thank you for being a part of my life."

What can I expect out of life as I grow older?

Life is worth living. The human experience is a gift. When you choose to focus on other things that are amazingly wonderful, you will recognize the gift that it is. Looking into the faces of your children, hearing their words and laughter, seeing the silly things they do. The warm embrace from your spouse or loved one, just when you need it most. The wonderful taste of food when you are hungry and the refreshment of a cool drink when your throat is parched. The feeling of a soft, warm bed at night at the end of a long day. The beauty and warmth of watching the sun rise over the horizon, or the majesty of how it colors the sky as it sets in the evening. These are just some of the things that enrich life if we pause long enough to enjoy them. In addition, life can be hard. Very hard. So many horrible things can happen that can appear unbearable at that moment. The loss of a child, spouse, or loved one. Financial ruin. Debilitating health issues. Becoming the victim of a crime. Deep adversity with someone in our lives, such as a coworker, neighbor, or even a family member. Life can hit hard, very hard. But it's not about how hard you get hit, it's about your ability to get back up and keep moving forward (Rocky Balboa). Seasons of life get harder while other seasons get easier. No matter what, be sure every day to look at the beauty and wonder that the day has to offer. That's why we call it "the present." Never forget that our time on earth is so temporary. We were created to live for all eternity with God. Prepare for that day, but don't miss what you have on this day. Life is worth living. It's a gift.

> **Life is worth living. It's a gift.**

In what way do you wish your life had turned out different?

I don't know that I can think of any ways that I wish my life had turned out different in any significant ways. I can't think of any specific things that I aspired to be or do when I was younger that never came to fruition later on in my life. I knew from an early age I wanted to go to college, get a degree in business, work in the field of business, get married, have a family, own a home, and have a good life. I guess you can call that pretty ordinary. Nothing ground-shaking or spectacular. It was what I wanted, a life of love that I can share with others. And I got that. I never wanted to be famous or a celebrity. I certainly didn't want all the chaos and turmoil that typically goes with that lifestyle. The only thing that comes to mind that would have been nice if it had turned out differently is if I had traveled more. By the time I was 21, I had traveled to 46 of the 50 States and nine countries. Since that time, I've only added four more countries. It would have been nice to travel more with you girls and with Mom, but I think that window of opportunity is pretty much closed by now. Despite that, I'm thankful for how my life has turned out. I have a wife (your mom) who I am so happy to be married to. It's been over 30 years, and we enjoy being with each other more now than ever before. I've never had to experience the devastation of divorce. I have two daughters whom I love so much and who love me back in their own unique way. I have my health, my home, I live in a place that I absolutely love. I have God in my life. I'm at peace with who I am. So, do I wish my life had turned out any different? Nah!

— Chapter 6 —
BECOMING A DAD

What is one thing you wish we'd done together that we haven't had a chance to yet?

It seems to me that this question would be better directed to you. What is one thing YOU wish we'd done together that we haven't had a chance yet? As mentioned earlier, I regret that we didn't travel, or vacation more than we did. Growing up, my family had done a lot of vacationing to places like Yosemite, Yellowstone, Zion National Park, Carlsbad Caverns, Grand Canyon, et cetera. We did lots of road trips and they were really fun. I never did that much with you girls. I don't know if you would have enjoyed trips like that or if you would have been bored. I know you enjoyed the trips to our timeshare in Indio. I just don't know if you would have enjoyed trying other things. I also realized that for you, wishing we had done something together might not have anything to do with vacationing. It might be something totally different for you. I'm so thankful for all the things that we did do together that we both enjoyed. College football games. Baseball games. Softball. Eating out. The vacations we took together as a family. Trips to Santa Barbara. I have so many great memories of our times together.

What was the scariest thing about fatherhood?

I guess it would be the unknown. Not knowing what to expect. Being a dad, there are so many uncertainties that you have to learn and figure out now that you have someone depending on you. It's one thing when you only have yourself to provide for and depend on. Where you go, what you do, what interests you and disinterests you. You then get married, and you have to bring two very different lives together to form a bond, a union in which two become one. That process is hard enough on its own. Now you bring a baby into this world, and you become a dad for as long as you both shall live. What do you do? How do you do it? It starts small. Little things, such as, what do I feed this child? How do I dress it? Is she too hot? Too cold? Is she sick? Is there anything wrong that I need to take action on? Later, you wonder about proper parenting. What do I teach my kid? How do I discipline? Where should I school them? What about their friends? What do I do if I don't know what to do? Every decision you make can highly be influenced by what you saw modeled in your own parents as you were growing up, whether good or bad. Then what makes things even scarier are the influences and experiences of your child that are outside of your reach. Is someone getting them into drugs? Exposing them to harmful things? Sexually assaulting them? Bullying them? Will they be abducted? Murdered? Physically harmed in some way? These are all scary things about fatherhood. Thankfully, we have the opportunity to be adopted by a Heavenly Father, our Creator God, who brings us into His family through Jesus, who helps us in our fatherhood journey.

Did you always know you wanted to become a dad?

Oh yes, without a doubt. Aside from that time I talked about earlier, when I was much younger and I didn't like kids, I knew I always wanted to be a dad. The opportunity to pour your love into another young human with the opportunity to receive that love back. Priceless! I remember a friend of mine I had when we were both in our 30s. I asked him and his wife if they thought about having kids. He said, "I know this sounds really awful, but we decided that we are too selfish to have kids and we don't want the responsibility or expense of raising them." I respected their honesty and decision. They were correct in acknowledging that there is a huge responsibility and expense to raising children. Yet, that was something I was willing to accept, and my how I'm so glad that I did!

How did you feel the first time you found out my mom was pregnant?

Well, as you know, she wasn't. So instead, I'll tell you how I felt when I found out your birth mother Sunni had chosen us to adopt you. "Wow! So I guess we're going to have a baby." I was equally shocked, scared, and excited. The shock was because Sunni was going to be our last birth mother interview, as we had planned on closing our adoption file with our attorney, as Mom and I felt that we weren't going to have kids after all. Scared, because our life as we knew it was going to change forever, and we didn't really know how that was going to look. Excited, because we wanted to have a child and become a family and you would be entering our lives in about six months. It only took a very short time for the shock and scare to go away, and I was nothing but excited!

What was one of our most special moments as father and child?

The most special moment for me is one that you were too young to remember, and that was when I laid eyes on you for the first time. You were only 20 minutes old, and they would only allow one person into the hospital nursery. I went in because I had been videotaping everything with a camera that my dad bought us. I remember looking at you and you were so beautiful. I was thinking to myself, "Wow, she's only 20 minutes old and my life will forever be changed." It wasn't a thought of regret or distress, but rather one of unknown excitement and anticipation. There were so many other special moments that we had together which come to mind. Putting you to bed at night and telling you/reading you stories. Taking you on camping trips. Goofing around at the grocery store with "Columbo Beans" and spraying you with the hose in the produce section. Getting you involved in softball, being on the dirt for all those practices, games, tournaments, and team videos. Of course, all the baseball games we went to and the college football games. But one of the most special times for me when you got older was the night you told us you were pregnant. You weren't married and you were so afraid. You were crying so hard, and my heart was broken for you. Not for me, I wasn't angry or upset. Rather, I felt such compassion for you. Mom and I cried along with you because we knew everything in your life just changed. You felt horrible because you thought you killed the CROP program because you did what I had taught you not to do. But I assured you that you hadn't killed CROP—you had actually validated it. I've always taught, as CROP teaches, that a parent's role is to raise their children well and then release them to make their own choices, knowing consequences can be short-term or lifelong. Getting pregnant before marriage carries lasting impact, and whether you kept the baby or chose adoption had to be your decision as a legal adult. I shared the beauty that can come from adoption—your birthmother's choice made our family possible—and reminded you that the next few years would be challenging either way. And then Anthony was born, and everything changed!

If you had to do fatherhood all over again, would you change anything? If so, what?

That's a really good question. For me, as a dad, I wanted to be a father. It was important for me to be involved in your life. That is a big reason why I changed careers when you were born. I used to work in the tech industry, and I traveled a lot for business. I had done that for 16 years, and I was used to it. Quite frankly, I enjoyed the travel and the work, and Mom was used to me being gone. But then you were born. I wanted to be a father in your life. I knew you needed your father, and Mom needed the help. So I made a drastic career change. I moved into a line of work where I would be home every night. It came with a price, though. My income dropped to less than half, and my benefits were not as good. It was a big hit financially to our household, but I was home with you and Mom every night. Was it worth it? Heck yeah! Would I do the same thing all over again? A thousand times out of a thousand! Being home gave us the ability to bond as a father and child and to grow together as a family. No amount of income or benefits could ever replace that. I felt that I always tried my best to become a good dad for you, and I can't recall ever doing anything to intentionally harm you. Other than a few small things that I mentioned earlier, such as traveling more often and getting you involved in sports earlier, I think I would do things pretty much the same.

> **I always tried my best to become a good dad.**

Give me your best advice about becoming a new parent.

Well, as I write this, you already are a new parent. You have a 4 1/2-year-old and a 19-month-old, so you probably would have better advice for a new parent than I would! Nevertheless, this is what I would share with you or anyone else:

Being a new parent is hard, but it's worth it.

There is no question that parenting requires a lot of sacrifice, and this is the hard part. Middle-of-the-night feedings, constant diaper changes. Fear that you're going to somehow break the child. Having to purchase and then pack up so much gear every time you go someplace. Then each stage of growth presents its own hardships, challenges, and expenses. But the "worth it" part so much outweighs the hard part. The cuteness of a newborn. Watching all the facial expressions. Delighting in the simple things, like watching the baby yawn, open its eyes, stretch, eat, burp. Each stage of growth presents its own joy. Rolling over, sitting up, lifting its head, crawling, walking, talking. Within our children, we have the opportunity to pour our love into them and receive that love back. I think that's a big reason God created humankind. He didn't need us. There was nothing He was lacking. The Father, Son, and Spirit are complete, lacking nothing. Yet He created us to pour Their perfect love into us. Everything around us, all that is created, He did for us. Just as we purchase and provide the best things that we can for our kids, God has done the same for us. He created us to love and to be loved. We each possess the power to give it and receive it. In the brokenness of this world, the issue of loving is probably the most damaged thing in our human experience due to sin. Thankfully, Jesus Christ set us free from sin and showed us perfect love.

What do you and I have most in common (features, traits, etc.) and how soon did you notice it?

Since you were adopted, we don't necessarily have any physical traits in common. What I have come to learn is that there is a difference between "Nature" and "Nurture." Nature is what is hardwired into you, passed down into your DNA from your birth mother and birth father. You don't change those things. You can't change those things. As you know, Mom and I were at the hospital the moment you were born, and we brought you home the very next day. You never lived with anyone else but us. Yet you have characteristics that you definitely got from your birth mother, not from us. Nurture is what you got from us. As a result, it took a longer time for me to observe things that we have in common as a result of nurturing or growing up in our household. What comes to mind is your love for college football and for baseball/softball. I have always loved going to games and watching them on TV, and so do you. I think our general attitude about life and the fact that we get over things and don't let stuff bother us too much is another thing we have in common. I've seen how CROP has forever bonded us and I believe it will play a much larger role in our future. Food! Loving food, eating food, and getting hangry when it's time to eat. That's definitely something we have in common. But as I think about it, I don't know if that's "Nature" or "Nurture." Oh well, let's go get some In 'N' Out, Chick-fil-A, or Tommy's Burger and talk about it...

Describe the bond you and I share.

I absolutely LOVE the bond that you and I share. It's one that I just sensed we were going to have for life the moment I laid eyes on you when you were only 20 minutes old. I knew it when I would hold you, I felt it whenever you would fall asleep in my arms. As you grew up, and I would hold you up in the air, or we would walk, and you would hold my hand. I always felt we had something special. That's why, if you remember, I would always call you my "Special Special." You weren't just special. You were "Special Special." Of course, you figured that out at a young age and used that to your advantage. I'm sure you remember the story when you were really little and you said to Mom, "Mommy, I can get anything I want from Daddy." Mom is thinking, "Oh, I've got to see this!" So she told you, "How do you get anything you want from Daddy?" You told her, "Watch!" Then you came into the other room where I was sitting, minding my own business and unaware of what was about to play out. You crawled into my lap, took my face into your hands and looked into my eyes while you said, "Daddy, you're so handsome and so brave and strong. I love you." And I said, "Thank you, honey. I love you too. Is there anything you need? Can I get you something?" You turned and looked at Mom with that grin of victory, and Mom says, "No way. I don't believe it!" And I, not knowing what's going on, said, "What?"

Tell me your secret thoughts about me as a kid in my most mischievous phase.

I wouldn't say that you were very mischievous as a kid. If you think you were, then that tells me you are very good at it. I can't recall having to rescue you or to discipline you very much because of situations that you got yourself into. But then again, I don't think I was very hard on you or controlling of your behavior. Granted, I didn't let you do anything you wanted to, and I didn't let you get away with everything. Rather, I recognized that doing and trying certain things while growing up is how you learn. Curiosity is natural, and while I never allowed you to drift into anything that was illegal or immoral, I feel that I did give you a fair amount of slack to try things out. Of course, I did know at times when you would fake being sick so that you didn't have to go to school. And you know the times I would take you to your room to spank your bottom, to discipline you for something, but I would tell you to fake cry when I slapped my thigh instead so that Mom would think I was spanking you. We would both laugh quietly because we didn't want Mom to know. I guess you could say I was complicit in some of your mischief.

[NOTE] Pretending to discipline your child in order to come across as the "cool" parent completely undermines the parenting process. Bad behaviors require real consequences. That is how we teach our children. By faking the spankings and laughing about it not only weakens the parental discipline process, but also shows disrespect to your spouse. For that, I apologize to both my wife Jan and to Kaylyn.

When or what time were you the proudest of me?

Every day of your life. There was never a time that I did not feel proud of you or proud to have you as my daughter. Proud to be your dad. However, one moment stands out way above any other time in your life. A time that may surprise you and a time that most people would not think to consider as a proud moment. That time was when you decided not to terminate your unplanned pregnancy with Anthony and to raise him as a single mom, despite the pressure you got from birth daddy. We knew this was a hard decision for you, especially as birth daddy chose not to stick around. Your heart was crushed, and I'm sure that the thought of raising a child on your own must have been daunting. However, you knew that you had our full support. With all of us living together, I'm sure you felt that you had a good shot at making it. Know this though. Even though we taught you and prepared you for the risks of an unplanned pregnancy outside of marriage, I can honestly say that not once, not even for a moment, did I ever feel embarrassed or ashamed of you. Life is filled with so many twists and turns that you have to be ready to adjust on a moment's notice. Some of these twists happen to us and others happened because of us. To me, what matters most is sticking by your family, helping each other out, loving one another in your hardship and through your hardship. And now seeing you as a wife and a mother of two boys, I'm very proud of how you have valued and cherished your own family the same way we do.

When you think of me, what's the first thing that comes to mind?

This question is a really tough one to answer because when I read it, my mind raced with so many things in a microsecond, each competing for that first thing. And now when I recall each thought that came to mind in that split moment, I have no idea which thought came first. So I'm going to have to deviate here from the question and answer it as "What are the first thing(s) that come to mind." I think of your face, your smile, your beautiful blue eyes, and your gorgeous long brown hair. I think of the first time I saw you when you were 20 minutes old. I think of how your hair stood straight up like a wave when you were a baby. How you used to have these overalls that we would dress you in when you were little, and I would pick you up with one hand by the back straps and hold you high in the air above my head and sing The Lion King song. I also think of all the times you would come to me when you were little and you would exclaim, "Daddy, Daddy, look at me!" while you then did some cute antic. Of course, driving you and your sister to school and singing The Phantom of the Opera songs. I think of teaching you to ride a bike and drive a car. I also think of all those days on the softball fields, watching you play and videotaping your games. Finally, I think of your transition into being a mom. You owned the responsibility and did everything that your boys needed from you. Despite the frequent hard times, you never complained or skirted your responsibilities. When I think of you, there is a whole lot that comes to mind.

When I was a child, what were your hopes and dreams for my life?

Well, I hope this doesn't sound terrible or expose a shortcoming in me as a father, but I honestly cannot think of any hopes and dreams that I had for your life when you were little. It was never important to me that you became what I wanted you to be. I didn't care if you liked what I liked, did what I did. It didn't matter if you went to college where I went, or even if you went to college at all. I know that you would be uniquely you and I wanted to nurture that for your good and the good of those around you. I never felt that I wanted a "mini-me." I guess the only hope (prayer) that I had for your life is that you would come to know God and have a personal relationship with Him through Jesus Christ. I lived the first 26 years of my life without that myself, so I know what it's like not to have one and to have one now. Life can be so hard, so confusing, so disappointing on its own. I don't know how anyone ever makes it through without God. He's the only one who is able to forgive, to release anyone from the guilt and shame that people carry as a result of their actions. He is the only one who offers purpose and clarity for life. I knew that you would face your own doubts, challenges, and confusion in your own life journey. My hope was that you would choose God as your friend to see you through.

Looking back, what were our craziest and funniest moments together?

USC football games. Angels baseball games. Teaching you to drive. Going to the grocery store. Softball games, both yours and mine. The trip to Lake Havasu. The CROP program and CROP graduation. The missions trip to Mexico. Schooling those teen boys in basketball on the cruise ship in Mexico. Our two-week trip to Hawaii. All our vacation trips to the timeshare in Indio. Ordering drive-through at Jack-in-the-Box. The day trip throughout Los Angeles. Smelling my breath and correctly guessing what I just ate. Airplane snacks and camping trips.

Be honest, what did I do that drove you crazy?

I am honest. I'm always honest. Which is why I cannot really think of anything that you did that drove me crazy. I think part of that is because I believe I'm pretty easygoing, and I don't let things really bother me. But the other part is that you never really did things that bugged me or were annoying. Mom may have a different answer than me, however. Yet you and I always had a good relationship where we would joke with one another and just have fun together. Still, we could be real and honest where we needed to be. So, nothing really drove me crazy that I can think of... Wait, I just thought of what did drive me crazy, what I guess my mind tried to block out to protect my sanity and my well-being. It was how messy you kept your bedroom and bathroom!

As I was growing up, what career path did you think I'd pursue?

A wife and mother? Success! I just didn't think it would be so young. To tell you the truth (as I said that I always do in the previous question), I never really thought of anything that you might pursue as a career. I knew that you always struggled with school, so I never expected that you would pursue a college education and select a major field of study. I never saw any interests or hobbies that attracted you that could eventually become a career. You did, however, always like boys, you loved cooking, and you were really good at babysitting and watching other people's kids. So that is why I figured you would become a stay-at-home wife and mother. That would become your career. Of all the things and choices that anyone could choose to pursue as a field of study or career, I think yours is the most important one ever. To take on the role of bringing children into this world and raising them to be productive and responsible members of society is, I think, the highest calling anyone can take. The future of our society depends on moms and dads doing that and doing that well. I see how you love and raise your boys, despite your fatigue and health challenges, and I know that you are living the role in life, the career path, that you were meant to. I'm so proud of you sweetheart!

What do you hope I learned from and what would you never want me to repeat?

It's better to marry first and then get pregnant? I say that with a humorous tone now, not with a tone of condemnation. Your two boys are so amazing, a true gift from God, and we are so happy that we are grandparents. You will have to admit, and you know it's true, that finding out you were pregnant was a very difficult thing for you. It was filled with fear and uncertainty. I'm sure a mixture of guilt, embarrassment, and shame as well. Confusion about what to do next. Who am I going to tell? How am I going to tell them? What will I say? How will they react? What will they think of me? This is not how pregnancy should be. It should be a happy and joy-filled occasion, one in which everyone celebrates with you. This is how God intended it to be: the excitement and anticipation of bringing a new life into this world. However, our family has truly seen how "all things work together for good for those who love God" (Romans 8:28). The blessing that those two boys have been in all of our lives can hardly be measured. Life is so filled with unexpected twists and turns. That is why having a strong faith and being surrounded by people who love and support you is so critical to have throughout your life. To be clear, I was NEVER angry, ashamed, or disappointed when you got pregnant. My heart just broke for you because I saw the anguish that you were in. I'm so thankful that we were able to be there for you.

How good of a job do you think you did as a dad?

I would give myself a B+. I think I fell short of an A-, A, or A+. However, I believe I was well above the average grade of a C. I think that the role of a dad is to do the best job possible in providing for the physical, mental, emotional, and spiritual well-being of his children. By doing so, he has equipped his children to be released from his care and launched out into the world to be a productive member of society. I look around and see how so many young adults are so angry, selfish, demanding, and emotionally fragile. They whine and complain, as though the world owes them something. People like this will never live a fulfilling, productive life if they continue in their behavior. They have been duped into a world narrative that robs them of joy and prevents them from filling their God-given potential. The world owes them nothing. It is up to each of us to determine what we desire and then pursue it, work for it. As a dad, my job has been to provide a warm, safe place for you to grow up in (physical needs), educate you academically and socially (mental needs), help you in processing emotional events and responses without contributing any harm (emotional needs), and guiding you to understanding and receiving the one true God into your life (spiritual needs). So looking back, yes, I would give myself a solid B+.

I could be the biggest brat when...

You would pick on your sister. I get it. Most older siblings pick on their younger ones at times, even seemingly tormenting them. My older brother did it to me, and you did it to your younger sister. You knew how to push her buttons, and you did it so often when Mom or I weren't looking. We always knew when you were at it when she would shriek and start crying loudly. It wasn't a cry of injury or discomfort. It was a cry of frustration. She didn't know how to defend herself, so eventually she learned to start hitting and punching you in her despair. When she hit you, you would back off, but then made it worse when you would laugh at her frustration. Thankfully, you both grew out of that phase and not only became loving sisters, but good friends, just as my brother and I did. Do you remember, "Twinkle, Twinkle, Little Star...?" That was bad, but I have to admit that I still laugh at that one.

What was the one thing I gave or give you, others can't?

Delight. That is the first word that came to mind to me. Delight. I was delighted when I saw you awake. I was delighted when I saw you sleeping. When you would crawl, when you would be learning to walk. I would delight in watching you eat, when you would play, when you were in your car seat in the back of my car, and you would suck your thumb with your right hand while pulling on the hair at the back of your head with your left hand. And now I delight in when I see you drive up into my driveway. When you come over to visit. When I come to your house, or you come to mine. When you FaceTime call us. I have never once had the thought or feeling of, "Ugh, it's her again." I have always been happy to see you and to hang out with you. To be clear, the word "delight" means "a high degree of pleasure or enjoyment; joy, satisfaction." That is how I always felt about you.

How did you pick my name? Did you almost name me something else, and what other names did you consider?

Kaylyn Leigh Martinez. That's it. There were no other ideas or considerations. We knew that this would be your name from the beginning. Now this was not your birth name. When you were born, your birth mother had given you the name Diana, which was one of her best friends at the time. That was the name printed on your birth certificate. When you were legally adopted by us and we went to court for the proceedings, at that time your birth certificate was changed along with your name, and you were listed as being naturally born to us. Your first name, Kaylyn, was easy. It was a blend of Mom's sister "Kay" and my sister "Lynda," who some people call "Lyn." Your middle name Leigh means "meadow." Mom picked it when she was going through a list of baby names. Mom was unable to have children, which was her lifelong dream since childhood. When she learned that her fate was permanent and irreversible, and there was nothing she could do about it, she descended into a three-year suicidal depression. She said she felt like she was lost in the deepest, darkest forest with no way out. Every time friends of ours announced they were pregnant, or a baby was born, it felt like a hard slap in the face from a low-hanging tree branch in that forest. Through counseling, she began to start feeling like she was emerging from that forest, until one day she felt like she actually stepped out of that deep, dark forest into a sunny meadow. Only then was she ready to take the next step in life, which was to become a family through adoption. That is why your middle name is "Leigh." You were the representation of that warm, sunny meadow that embraced Mom.

What was the one thing you wish you knew before becoming a father?

Well, quite frankly, nothing really comes to mind. I was almost 38 years old when you were born, and we had earnestly been looking for a baby to adopt, so I don't think that I wasn't ready or caught off guard. I had plenty of years observing other people as they stepped into fatherhood, so I kind of knew what to expect. Likewise, since I wasn't a teenager or in my young 20s when you were born, I had plenty of time to mature myself and be more established in my career, owning a home and being comfortable in our financial situation. Most importantly, Mom and I had been married for almost six years by the time you were born, so we had the time we needed to establish a strong foundation in our own relationship so that we were best prepared to welcome you into our family. I really don't think anything about fatherhood caught me off guard.

Tell me about myself as an infant. What funny story should I know that happened when I was really young?

You were an easy child. A very easy child. You hardly ever cried, you rarely fussed. In fact, people would always comment to us, "This is not a normal baby. How did you get such an easy baby? Be careful, your next one probably won't be as easy. Can I take her? Do you need a babysitter? I'll watch her anytime you need." Perhaps you being such an easy child was part of God's reward to us for having to go through what we went through in order to have children. Regardless of the reason, we were so thankful that you were an easy child. I think the funniest thing for me about you was the way your hair used to stand straight up like a wave. You, and your sister like you, were born with very full, thick heads of hair. Neither of you were ever baldies. When you turned about three months old, and for the next few months, your hair pointed straight up. It didn't matter how we brushed it or styled it; your hair went straight up in the air. It was very cute.

Describe my terrible twos.

Your twos were not terrible. Your threes were. I remember Mom and I commenting to one another several times, "What's up with the terrible twos lore? This is really easy." And then you turned three. Oh my, there it is. Throwing little tantrums. Making a mess of everything. Talking back. In reality, very normal things for kids around this age. Thankfully, nothing that was unbearable. You were still a pretty easy kid. However, your favorite words became "me" and "mine." You were pretty enamored with yourself. Since you grew up before the days of streaming media on demand (yes, you did survive those prehistoric ancient dark days), if you wanted to watch a movie, we would have to play a video on a VCR tape player. Oftentimes when I would ask you if you wanted to watch a video, you would shout out, "I want Kaylyn video." I would put in a tape that I had recorded of you doing something and you would just sit there, mesmerized as you watched yourself on tape. When the video was over, you'd say "Again!" and I would rewind the tape and play it for you. I will say though, that it never got old or boring for me. I always thought that it was really cute, because truth be told, I liked watching Kaylyn videos too!

> Your twos were not terrible. Your threes were.

When I have kids, what karma do you hope comes back to me? What hellishness did I put you through?

I don't wish any hellishness on you. Why would I want that? Just as I always wanted good things for you and your sister in your lives, I want the same thing for your kids. (Maybe a little bit more for them.) Grandchildren are so amazingly wonderful, and they are God's reward for surviving your kids when they were teenagers! It is funny though, how you have told me that you are so glad that you have boys, because you don't think you could handle a girl that turned out just like you. I never quite understood that because I don't think you were anywhere near as bad as you think you were. But maybe there were some more things about you that we didn't know about? The truth is, parenting is hard. It doesn't matter if you're a good parent or a bad parent, a good kid or a bad kid. The process of raising a child is hard. Likewise, the process of being raised as a child is hard as well. Beginning at the age of about 10 or 11 and continuing on from there, a child really starts to step into their own uniqueness and wants to exercise their own will. They become smarter, even to the point that they sometimes think they are smarter than their own parents. They think that so much of what their parents do is dumb, and they want to be free of their parents. But they can't be. They are still so much more dependent on their parents as they go through their teen years. This is when it gets harder. When it does, just hang in there. Always remind yourself that you are the adult and your children's brains are still forming. They are still learning how to deal with their emotions. Be patient, be consistent, be involved, and everything will be just fine. Even if you do wind up having a daughter!

What do you think is my best personality trait, and who did I get it from?

Hmm. That's a tough one. Your best? Well, the first thing that comes to mind is that you are tough. Ever since you were a little girl, you rarely allowed hurt or disappointment to simmer. You would cry for a short period of time and then you would press forward with resolve and determination. You've carried a lot of that into adulthood. You value family and the family relationship, so you often call just to talk and to see how we are doing (you get that from Mom mostly, and secondly from me). I always liked how you had confidence in yourself in many areas, whether it was in softball, cooking, or other areas of your life. You have a wittiness about yourself, and you are quick with your humor and know how to make people laugh (you definitely got that from me!). Here's the thing to keep in mind: every person has personality traits that either bring others up or pull them down. When we walk into a room, does the mood go up or is the air sucked out of the room? We each have the power to influence others by leaning into the power of our best personality traits, while learning to self-control our less desirable ones. Life is not intended to be lived for our own self-indulgence and gratification, but to help lift others up and to make our corner of the world a better place. That is where the richness, joy, and fulfillment of life truly come from.

What birthday of mine stands out as most special? Why?

That's kind of a hard one because unfortunately, it's hard for me to remember any birthdays. Not just yours, but Mom's, mine, or your sister's. Certainly, your first birthday is an easy one to remember. That was when you tasted sugar for the first time when we fed you your birthday cake. You weren't really sure about it at first, but as you ate more of it, you really grew to like it. I guess the one that does stand out most was your 13th birthday. That was the one in which I shared with you that you are about to step into a life stage where everything is going to change. You were going to really start developing into an independent thinker, and the world was going to start throwing a lot of things your way, many of them harmful, and you were going to have to make a decision about them. I shared with you how many cultures recognize this, and that they have a rite-of-passage that boys and girls go through. I wanted to take you through one and to prepare you for the decisions you would be faced with, that only you can make. I asked you if you would like me to do that for you, and you said "yes." That is what eventually became CROP. Through that, we now have the opportunity to impact numerous teens and families around the world.

What is your most treasured memory of just you and me?

Your CROP graduation. Celebrating the culmination of this extensive, parent-led mentorship program, and being able to pray my blessing over you. This was a coming-out event for you. That is, I was able to declare that I did my part to prepare you for the ways of the world and the decisions you would have to make, both good and bad, and that I released you to your decisions. Granted, my role as your father was not complete. As long as we both have breath in our lungs, I'm willing to guide and mentor you as much as you're willing to receive it. The CROP graduation for me represented a milestone in your life. It represented your first steps into adulthood and adult responsibilities. It also recalibrated my compass in my role as your dad. I was no longer to treat you as a child, telling you where to go or what to do. Rather, it set a new course in our relationship. I was now more of a coach; someone who explained to you that you are now playing a new game called the Game of Life. This was a game that only you could play. I couldn't be on that playing field with you. But as a coach, I could help explain the rules to you, let you know what's coming at you. I could celebrate your victories with you while helping to pick you up in your defeats. I could see things differently from the sidelines that you couldn't see because you would be in the midst of the struggle, emotion, and sweat of the game. My prayer has always been that you would seek guidance, you would want to do well in this difficult life game, and that you/we would enjoy many more victories than we would defeats.

Looking back on all the bad things I did as a child, which one secretly made you laugh?

Well, as I said previously, you did not do a lot of bad things as a child. It's either because you just didn't do them or because I don't want to remember! There were some things you did that made me chuckle. For example, faking that you were sick or that your throat was sore so that you wouldn't have to go to school. I knew most of the time when it was fake and when it was real. But I figured if you didn't want to go to school on any particular day, there was a reason for it, and missing a day of school here or there wasn't going to wreck your life. (I'm sure some of those missed sick days were because of simple laziness. Oh well.) But the thing that secretly made me laugh, and you too, were the fake spankings. I knew you hated receiving spankings, and you would genuinely cry deeply when you knew you were getting one. Yet sometimes I would let it slide even if you deserved to get one, and Mom was expecting me to impose discipline that you deserved. On occasion, and not as often as your mom or sister believes, I would take you into your room and tell you to start crying whenever I slapped my thigh real hard. It sounded like a spanking, and your tears made it seem real. Mom thought you were getting the discipline that you deserved, all the while that you and I were secretly laughing in the other room. Perhaps I thought that this helped me to be a good dad to you. Yet as I think about it, I probably shouldn't have done that.

[NOTE] Pretending to discipline your child in order to come across as the "cool" parent completely undermines the parenting process. Bad behaviors require real consequences. That is how we teach our children. By faking the spankings and laughing about it not only weakens the parental discipline process, but also shows disrespect to your spouse. For that, I apologize to both my wife Jan and to Kaylyn.

How did you feel the first time you saw me after I was born?

It was a combination of wonder, fear, delight, and responsibility. Wonder, in the fact that, "Wow, I'm a dad, this is crazy. We wanted a child and now we have one." Fear, in that I didn't know what to do. I had no idea what the future would hold. I stepped into something unknown: Fatherhood. Would I have what it takes to raise a child and not screw up that child's life? Delight, in that you were such a precious little baby. You know, by having children of your own, that little babies can be so cute and adorable and every little face they make or squeal they utter is so precious. And responsibility, in that I knew from that moment forward that I was going to have a huge part in raising you, feeding you, clothing and sheltering you, educating you, guiding you and comforting you. This was on me now, along with your mom, of course, to care after this little creature that God brought to us via your birth mother. Has it been difficult? At times, yes. Sometimes more than others. Was it worth it? Oh, yes! Without a doubt. Given the choice to do it again or not, I would do so 1000 times out of 1000. You and your sister have been such a blessing to my life. I would not want it any other way.

How are we the most different?

You're pretty and I'm not? I don't know. That's the first thing that came to mind. You have long, thick, beautiful hair and I... oh, forget it! I want to say that the biggest difference is that I like things to be clean, orderly, and picked up. I like my house, my car, and my living spaces looking very tidy. Whenever I would be at home alone for a few days or more, the first thing I would do is clean the entire house and enjoy the look and feeling of tidiness. However, it's really hard to keep a home clean when there are multiple people living there. The truth is, I contribute my share of messiness when others are around. I was just commenting to Mom recently that when you bring the boys over, the house gets turned upside down in about 45 minutes. But they are little boys, and that's what little boys do. Given the choice between having the place a mess with them here or having it clean without, I would choose you and them being here every time! That is the difference between a house and a home. A house is something to look at, whereas a home is a place you create memories in. Stuff is just stuff and messy can always be cleaned up. But you can't bring back family once they are gone.

> **A house is something to look at, whereas a home is a place you create memories in.**

Tell me about one of my most embarrassing moments in school and how we got through it together.

OK, on this one I could not really come up with anything. In fact, I asked both you and Mom for help on this question, and neither of you could think of anything either. So I'm going to write about the only thing that came to mind to me. That is, leaving you behind when you weren't ready for school in the morning. Despite knowing the time we needed to leave the house in order to get you and your sister to school on time, you often ran behind and would not be ready in time. This really irritated your sister and me because it would cause her to be late for her first class and she would get in trouble for it. I then told you that if you weren't ready in time, we would leave without you. Well, I'm sure your initial thought was, "Cool, I won't have to go to school that day." I told you your consequence was that you would have to clean the house during the day. No TV, no phone, and you would have to go to each teacher the following day and apologize for missing school simply because you weren't ready in time. There were times when I was pulling the car out of the driveway, and you would come running out. I recall a time or two when I had driven down the street and I saw you run out into the street to wave me down via my rearview mirror. And then there were the times that you never came out, and we left without you. However, there is one thing I'm not really clear on. Did I ever enforce those consequences?

What was the hardest talk you ever had to have with me?

Easy answer, hard talk. When you told us that you were pregnant. I'm certain that will be a conversation and a night that none of us will ever forget. I remember seeing the fear and shame in your eyes, through your tears. You probably had no idea how Mom or I would respond, perhaps thinking the worst. My heart absolutely broke for you, not because of any anger or disappointment on our part, but because I knew the distress that you were in. We cried with you, we tried to comfort you, and we tried to assure you that everything will be OK. There would have to be a difficult decision to make, one that did not have to be made that night but would still need to be made: either keep and raise the baby or place the baby for adoption. Either decision will be difficult, as they both have lifelong implications. I shared with you how adoption is a loving option, as your birth mother chose to go to term with you in her unplanned pregnancy, and now, as a result of her choice, we are a family. However, we are a family that believes in and values life, so terminating the pregnancy was not an option. The conversations we had with you late into that night, as well as being with you when you had to talk to baby daddy, were very difficult. I will say, though, that I felt equipped to face that moment and to guide our family through it without shrinking back from it. My beliefs (God) determine my values (Life) and my values dictate my actions (protect you and the life of your baby). I don't say this pridefully, but with humble confidence: I don't know how that discussion and the ensuing months could have gone better. Despite the hardship and broken heart you had to endure at that time, what has become our reward for endurance and obedience? Your son, my grandson.

Did you pass down any advice or techniques that your dad, my grandfather, gave you?

I'm sure there have been plenty, whether passively or intentionally. Numerous things come to mind. Social events, parties, get-togethers with friends, etc. Valuing family relationships is something I hope we passed on to you. Having a sense of humor, working hard, taking personal responsibility for your words and actions. These are all things that I received that I hope got passed on. One thing that I don't know that may have passed on is the value and commitment to education. What I mean by that is that I knew from a young age that I wanted to go to college and then start a business career. My brother did as well, and my sister too. Yet school was never much of a thing for you and your sister. You did what you needed to do to graduate high school, as did your sister, and you didn't have college aspirations. There is no fault in that and there is nothing wrong with that in itself. Quite frankly, with what college has become in our country, I'm glad you didn't. However, continuing to educate yourself in personal interests and life skills is so important. These are the things that really matter most at your current life stage. Not science, math, history, or geography. Rather, things that will help you be a better wife, mother, friend, and person. This world needs way more great people than what we currently have, and you can be one of those if you continually work on improving yourself. This comes from self-education.

What punishment was the hardest to give me and why?

I can't think of the hardest punishment I gave you, but I'm happy to tell you about my favorite! I learned it from a course that I took on parenting (remember what I just wrote on the importance of continually educating yourself?) called The Parent Project. This particular strategy was about how to get your kids to do something that you want them to do by tying it to something that they want to do. Here's how it works. You want your kid to clean their room or do the dishes. Your kid wants to go to the movies or hang out with their friends. When they ask if they can go, you say, "Sounds fun! Absolutely, you can go as soon as you finish cleaning your room/doing the dishes. Take as much time as you'd like. Let me know when you're done so that I can check your work. Then you're free to go. There's no rush." Every time I did that, you got your work done faster and better than at any other time. I realize this was not an actual punishment, but rather a strategy to ensure that we both got what we wanted so that I didn't have to punish you. Another thing I liked to do was to give you your choice of work or consequences by making sure that I always gave you an option that was much worse than what I actually wanted you to do. For example, I'd want you to clean your bathroom, so I'd give you the choice of either cleaning your bathroom or vacuuming the entire house and scrubbing all the toilets. You would choose your bathroom every time, which is what I wanted you to do in the first place. Remember these and try them on your kids. They work really well.

Describe our relationship in your own words.

Happy. Pleased. Content. Delighted. Satisfying. Enjoyable. Proud. Fulfilling. Love. Many words describe how I feel our relationship is. As a dad who really wanted kids and looked forward to all the duties and responsibilities that fatherhood requires, I have found fulfillment in our relationship. I never felt that we had any seasons in our lives where we were at odds with one another. Certainly, I know we had our moments when you were angry or upset with me or me with you. But these moments never seemed to last very long. Funny, when it came to this page in the journal, I happened to read the quote at the bottom of the page before I read the question at the top. It struck me deeply how true that statement is. A child's greatest need from a father is protection. Protection from danger, protection from fear, protection from hunger, lack of self-worth, and insecurity. Protection from allowing the culture to define who they are rather than helping them know who God thinks they are. I think of so many successful people who accomplished great personal and financial success in their effort to obtain validation and acceptance from a father who was never able to offer that. They would easily trade all that they achieved, to hear their fathers say, even once, "I love you, my son/my daughter. I'm proud of you." My hope for you has always been that even if you were poor in worldly wealth, you would be rich in your relationship with God and me.

> "I cannot think of any need in childhood as strong as the need for father's protection."
> —Sigmund Freud

What things did you have to learn as you went along? Who did you regularly call for advice on being a father?

As I mentioned earlier, I think I had an advantage over many dads because I did not become a father until I was almost 38 years old. I had the advantage of being more emotionally mature, financially stable, and wiser as a result of observing other dads. Yet you can only be so prepared because the only way to work through real life challenges is to experience them. So my go-to sources for learning about being a dad included my own father, mother, sister, and wife. I'll also include my men's Saturday morning Bible study group, the Bible itself, and numerous classes and workshops that I attended over the years. I think the hardest thing that I had to learn as a father did not involve you, but rather your sister. As you know, she and I had great difficulties in our relationship. We were at odds with one another for many years. So many times, I felt like giving up on her and tapping out on being her dad. My mind replayed over and over the words that I wanted to say to her, comments that I felt totally justified to say to her, which were in response to how hurt I felt by her, and those words would have cut her deeply. Yet I knew that if I ever allowed those words to leave my lips, I could never take them back. I had to remind myself that I was the adult parent, she was the teen, and I needed to exercise maturity. I'm so glad that I did because I realize her needs are very different from yours, and by my patience and adjusting to this reality, our relationship is much better today.

What was the greatest invention for dads, in your opinion?

Beer? Actually, I always said that woman was God's greatest invention because of all the things that woman means to mankind. But woman is not an invention, she is a creation, just like man. I'm thinking hard about an honest answer to this question: an invention that is dad-specific, not just for men in general. As I try to expand my thoughts across so many options, only one thing is stuck in my head that keeps coming back to mind over and over: disposable diapers. Yup, my dad generation is the first one to not have to deal with washable cloth diapers. If I had to deal with cloth diapers, either I would never have changed diapers or else I would have thrown up every time.

What was the one thing you worried about the most where I was concerned?

It's the same concern I still have for you, I always will have, and that I have for your sister as well: that you would walk away from your faith. I worry that you will get lazy, that you will become self-indulgent, that you will be deceived to turn away from the one and only true God that created you, loves you and wants to walk life's journey with you. But you must want Him. You must draw near to Him. Only you can determine the quality of your relationship with Him. If God ever seems distant to you, it's not because He moved. He will always remain as close to you as you allow Him. I really don't know how people make it through life without having God in their life.

What moments as a father made you laugh the most?

I would say it's that period between when you were 18 months to four years old. That is the age when a child's true personality starts to play out. Their learning accelerates as they experience the world around them. They are learning new words as their speech develops and there were so many times I would stop in my tracks and say, "Wait, did you see that? Did you hear what she just said? Where did she get that from?" It really is a cute time. Those were also the times when I would put you to bed. I would either read you stories or I would make them up. I wanted you to fall asleep so that I could go back downstairs to spend time with Mom or watch some TV with her. Quite frequently, Mom would look up and see you coming down the stairs. She would say, "Where's Daddy?" You would say, "He's sleeping in my bed." My reading to you and storytelling at bedtime was very effective, just not on the person it was intended for.

What life lesson do you feel is most important for me to learn?

There are so many choices, so many things for me to point to. I've covered so much already in this journal to you. As a dad who loves his kids, I always want the best for you. But the best doesn't mean the easiest. I've seen so many parents who, perhaps with good intentions, give and do everything for their kids. They give them whatever they want, they bail them out of trouble, they never have them work for anything, and they tolerate any behavior. The parent doesn't realize that this actually wrecks their kids. It teaches them to be a dependent, self-indulgent, immature brat who will really struggle living on their own in the real world. That is why the lesson that I feel is most important for you to learn is perseverance. Perseverance means you keep going on, no matter what obstacles or setbacks you encounter. Life is filled with so many disappointments and defeats. People will disappoint you, betray you, even leave you. Many times, it's the people that are closest to you. There will be times in your life when you will feel totally lost, confused and hopeless. You will be frozen in fear because you won't know what to do next. Anxiety and panic may set in. This is when you need to persevere. This is when you need to learn to lean into God and to those who love you. This is how you get through. You weren't meant to live your life alone.

Who or what was your biggest helper as a dad?

Mom. Without a doubt. No question, no pondering, no other choices. Your mother. As you personally know by now, having your own kids, parenting is extremely difficult and demanding. There is a heavy price to pay in terms of time, energy, emotion, and financially when you are a parent. This is not a complaint, but rather a statement. There is a reason that God's plan is for a child to have both a mother and father in their life. The child needs that for their growth and well-being, and the parents need each other to help bear the load. However, now more than ever, we are seeing families without both parents present and available in the household. Sometimes the parent abandons their responsibility. Divorce takes place. A parent dies. And perhaps worst of all is the parent that is physically present but is mentally or emotionally detached. My heart truly breaks for the young man and young lady who did not have a parent or parents available to them. Where do they go for guidance, wisdom, help, and acceptance? I believe there are millions of men and women who are walking wounded, who never received the love and validation that each young person needs. That is why your mom has clearly been the biggest helper for me as a dad. We remain in alignment, though not always in agreement, in our commitment to raising you girls in the manner we felt was best for you.

What have you always tried to protect me from?

Danger. Danger from violence. Danger from drugs. Danger from unhealthy relationships in your life. The life journey demands that we all experience certain things that could be harmful to us. Some are the result of poor decisions we make, and some are because we happen to be in the wrong place at the wrong time due to no fault of our own. My mind cannot even comprehend the anguish I would endure if something evil and terrible happened to one of you girls. I remember a long time ago, watching a program well before I was married or a dad, where a young girl was raped and murdered by a selfish, evil man. Eventually the mother committed suicide because she could not cope with what happened. I didn't understand that then, but I do now.

As a father, what did you want more of, that you never had enough of?

I had always wanted more kids. I wanted three or four. As an adult, I've had a true love for kids and I'm always happy when I'm around them. Believe it or not, I like the noise and the messiness that comes from kids (although I don't like the diapers!). That's why I've so often told many of your and your sister's friends that I want to adopt them. That's why I would drive the van after your softball games and tell all the girls, "Let's have a screaming contest!" while Mom drove separately and peacefully alone in another car. But God's plan was for us to just have two, and yet, because of who you both are, my life is still full.

In what ways was fatherhood not all it was cracked up to be?

For me, I don't have an answer for this question. It implies that somewhere along the way, fatherhood is a letdown, a disappointment. I'm sure that for countless numbers of dads, they actually feel this way. Worse yet, they've probably even told that to their son or daughter. "You're such a disappointment. You're a real letdown. You're such a failure and I'm ashamed to even call you my son (or daughter). Fatherhood is not cracked up to be what it seems. You should never have kids." Wow. Can you imagine hearing those words from your own dad? How does someone ever recover from that mark that is left on their life? Not one person on this earth had a choice in who their father is. Not one. But here's the good news. We all have a choice in who we invite into our life to be the father figure that we need. It can be a neighbor, a friend's father, a pastor, a coworker, another family member. It can be a mentor who speaks, writes, and publishes fatherly advice, a person that you will never meet. There are still plenty of people in this world who have a real heart to be a guiding voice through their journey of life. Most importantly, we have the open invitation into a relationship with our Heavenly Father. The one who created us and knows our every thought and need. He beckons us to find forgiveness, acceptance, and restoration through a relationship with Him, but He never forces His way into our life. Every human father on earth has the capacity to wound their kid, even deeply. Only the heavenly Father is able to heal those wounds and to restore a wounded heart back to health.

Did having a child/children stand in the way of your dreams?

Having children was my dream. Being married to the same woman for as long as we both shall live was my dream. Raising my kids to prepare them to be released positively into the world has always been my dream. Too many times people focus their dreams on success in their career, in becoming well-known and idolized and gaining worldly possessions, positions of power and influence, or traveling the world. For what? At what expense? I guess it's one thing if you're single to pursue these things, or if you are married and you both want those things. Yet here's the irony. Someone can work years, even decades to pursue those worldly dreams, only to have it all taken away from them in just one moment. Then what? Who are they? What are they? Where is their identity?

> **Having children was my dream.**

There are too many celebrities to name who found themselves in this predicament, which led them down the rabbit hole of substance abuse, depression, and suicide. Tragic. A wasted life. But being a good husband? Being a good father? That is something that can never be taken from me. All the pleasures, power, and possessions that this world has to entice me with can be taken from me. You cannot take from me that I did what I could to be the best husband possible for my wife and the best father possible for my kids.

Were you afraid of becoming like your father?

No. I wanted to become like my father plus more. I find it interesting that this question would be in this journal. It implies that a father was a bad experience and that nobody wants to grow up and become like their father. While I'm certain that this is the case for many people, I have no idea what the percentages are of good dad or bad dad experiences. I'm very grateful that I had a good dad experience. I have many fond memories of my dad when I was growing up. I feel that he gave me the time and encouragement that I needed. He was fair in his discipline (yep, I deserved every punishment that I received). He provided well for the family, and he remained committed to my mom. They are only two months away from celebrating their 68th wedding anniversary as I write this. There are many characteristics of my dad that I wanted to adopt. There were also other ones that I wanted to infuse into my relationship with my kids. For example, being able to have open and honest conversations on any life issue, especially the difficult ones. That is, in part, how CROP came to be. Living my faith boldly and out loud. Being active in engaging others in spiritual conversations. This is another way that I wanted to be more. I also changed my career path shortly after you were born so that I could be home every night, whereas my previous career had me traveling constantly. I hope these decisions wound up being of value to you.

What have you always wanted to ask me but never did?

Was I good, dad? If so, why? If not, why not? What makes a good dad? What do young teens need from their father? Their mother? When you think back upon the many friends you had in junior high and high school, what did they need from their parents that they didn't get? What did their parents do that made them very upset? How do the needs of a young person change regarding their parents when they transition from their teen years to a young adult in their 20s? I speak so often about the negative pressures of culture for young people to make poor, self-destructive choices. What were some of the real pressures you faced when you were a teen that parents should be more aware of? Were there times in your life where you were truly terrified about something, and you didn't know where to go or what to do for help? What would you say to a person, whether teen or adult, that either has an unhealthy relationship with their parent or parents, or has no relationship at all, and they feel like something is missing in their life? Was there or is there anything that you needed from me that you didn't get (other than money)? I think many parents, if not most, try to do a good job raising their kids, but there's often no conduit for offering feedback without things coming across as critical or confrontational. If these avenues of communication between parent and teen could be opened up, we'd have much stronger families and more well-adjusted people in this world.

What do you think is the most important role/task of a father?

To love his wife and remain faithful to her. The marriage between a husband and wife is a very unique relationship unlike any other. It's the only one in which two people become one flesh, one union, through the bond of matrimony. "For better or worse, rich or poor, sickness or health" is a covenant made until death parts that union. I believe that the number one thing a child needs from their parents is the security of knowing that their parents will stay together, will work things out no matter what. And I believe the father has the primary responsibility of doing everything he can to make that happen. A husband needs to learn how to love his wife, and a wife needs to learn how to respect her husband. These are the foundations for successful marriage. When kids see their parents working through the challenges in life, owning their own mistakes, confessing when wrong, and forgiving when being wronged, sticking to their commitment to marriage even when they don't feel like it, this is the best thing we can teach our kids and pass down to them. I believe that a boy will mostly become the man he saw modeled in his father, and a girl will be drawn to the type of man she saw modeled in her father, whether good or bad. Men need to rise up and to take the mantle of responsibility to be the husband that his wife needs, and the father that his children need. When a man leads his family in the way he was intended to, lives are so much richer, and society is so much better. My prayer is that I would be faithful to do my part so that one day I can hear "Well done!"

Letter from My Dad (Mark)

In October 1977 I went away on a weekend retreat for teenagers called "Youth Encounter". The retreat focused on helping young people examine their family, their faith, their relationships around them, and their purpose for existing. It was a pretty intense weekend, with lots of learning about love and the true things that matter in life. Leading up to the weekend, family members of each participant hand write a letter to the teen that is away on the encounter. The letter is an expression of each family members' thoughts and feelings about the participant. The letters are presented to the participants on the last day of the weekend encounter, shortly before their family members welcome them back live when they come to pick them up from the retreat location. It's a really emotional experience, to say the least. I don't know if Youth Encounter is still around, or how it might be different than when I went through it at the age of 17. Nevertheless, I do know that my father's letter to me had a deep impact on my self-worth and the security I felt in him as my dad. I'd like to share his letter to me with you.

My Son, My Son, My Son:

I've been praying that you had a good weekend. I'm sure that you've been busy since Friday, probably very tired and probably very happy.

You've been given a lot to think about this weekend. Some of it has caused you to think and feel deeply and some of it has not affected you too much. During this period, I would like to tell you how I feel. I am very happy that you decided to attend Youth Encounter. I'm sure that you have gained from the experience and are a better man for it. As I have always told you, you always gain and learn from new experiences - even if they are not pleasant. The important thing is that you learn from the exposure, and you profit from it.

Mark, I am very proud of you and love you very much. You have developed into a fine young man. You have a good head on your shoulders, you have a mature attitude, and you are still growing intellectually.

There have been times in the past (and probably in the future) where I have had to discipline you in one way or another. I'm sure that many times you felt that you were punished unjustly, and maybe sometimes you were. However, I want you to understand that whenever I administered discipline to you it's for a purpose - that of attempting to help you in your development. During these times, I always want you to remember that I love you and I always will.

It is hard to explain the love I have for you. You may think that you know what love is, and you have probably experienced some of it: however, it is nothing compared to the love I have for you monkeys*.

In the future when you get married and have kids (in that order!) stop and look at them deeply. You will experience a love for your kids that will be beyond anything you have ever experienced or are able to explain - that will be true love. Also, think back on this weekend and on this letter and how I have attempted to express my love for you. It is so deep and different that you can't explain it on paper - it's just there!

You are smart, ambitious and confident. You know what you want and are willing to work and study hard for it. It will be a long, hard pull to achieve your goals and I want you to know that I will help you in every way I can. You can depend on me for help or counsel at any time now or in the future. All you have to do is ask. As a matter of fact, you may get some of it even if you don't ask!

I am especially proud of you during your "special weekend" and my love and prayers have been with you all during this time. I can hardly wait to see you.

Love, Dad

*"monkeys" is the little love term that my dad used to refer often to us kids. It was never used as a derogatory name.

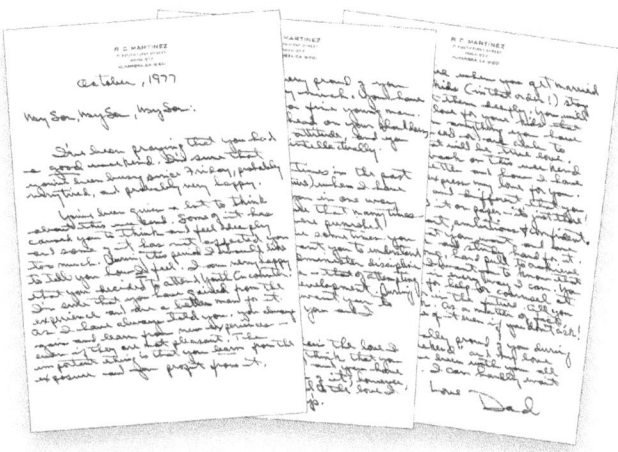

Post Journal Comments

I make several statements about girls, dating, being good-looking, etc. This is how I always kid around with my daughter. I am not so full of myself that I really believe that I'm something that I'm not. When you read these statements, I want to be clear that I make them mostly for the humor that I know my daughter will see in them.

I make some references to light alcohol and drug usage. I'm so thankful that I have never had a problem with alcoholism or drug addiction. Let me be clear here: I do not recommend the use of alcohol or illegal drugs. Some people are capable of handling alcohol, and some are not. Similarly, nothing good ever comes out of the use of illegal drugs. Besides, they are illegal, so that alone should be the reason not to use them. I don't want anyone to ever read, "Well, Mark experimented with some, so I'll wind up being okay." Not a good argument. I've known so many people throughout my life who have had serious addictions with things like tobacco, alcohol, drugs, and pornography. This is why I teach in the CROP classes that substance abuse is a no-win situation, and it's best not to ever get started.

On the question of what event brought the most emotional pain in my life, I reference an event I went through having to do with church. Sometimes it seems whenever there is a division among people of the same faith, it can be much harder to contend with. Faith should be a common denominator which brings us together, not bitterly divides us. However, that is not always so. Some might look at this, perhaps, as a reason not to participate in spiritual matters or fellowship with others. They may feel justified in maintaining a certain isolation in what they believe and how they practice it. For me, my experience was not cause for me to recoil in my involvement in church. I believe there is a spiritual battle that we are all involved in, no matter what we choose or choose not to believe in. In combat, where is the fighting the fiercest? The closer you get to the front lines. When I was on staff at church, that was one of the front lines where spiritual battle takes place. Recognizing this, I was and currently am in no position to surrender and tap out of the war. Rather, take time to heal from the wounds and get back into the fight. There is a very real enemy who also wants to take out my family and my friends, and I need to heed my call to arms to stand in the gap for them, as well as for others that I've yet to meet.

Thoughts About the Topic of Dating (from Mark)

Throughout this journal, I have made several references to my history on dating. I was 12 years old when I started being interested in girls and I was 14 when I started dating. I liked girls. I liked a variety of girls. I liked several types of girls. It seems the more I got, the more I wanted.

I know, this may immediately come across as "objectifying" girls. In reality, it was. In my young, teenage, hormone-infused brain, girls became a "thing" for me, something to pursue. Anytime I went anywhere, whether to a party, a wedding, a vacation, or school, I was always on the lookout for a girl that would catch my eye, and I would try to get her to like me, to be interested in me. I called this "the thrill of the hunt." Sometimes I was "victorious," but more often than not I wasn't.

I can't say that I was ever an alcoholic, a drug addict, a sex addict, or anything else like that. However, if you could describe an addict as someone who is constantly thinking about an object of desire and is always looking for a way to get that thing, then I guess I could have been referred to as a "girl addict." For me, the victory was in getting them to choose me as their "object of interest" at that moment.

Juvenile? Self-indulgent? Selfish? Of course. I was a teen boy who thought most about myself and what I wanted. This was my life in my high school and college years, and to some extent it continued into my young adult years, prior to getting married. Most of my dating relationships lasted between 2 – 6 months, rarely any longer than that, because I wanted to move on to the "next thing." Thankfully, I've grown out of that (truly, I have). However, my actions did leave a wake of harm to others, as well as myself.

I still recall the times I told someone I would call them, and I didn't. The times that I was able to get someone to kiss me (which I considered my "trophy"), and then I would move on from them. I recall the times I would be dating two different girls at the same time and then they found out about it (which quickly turned in to me dating zero). I know that I was the cause of letdown, heartbreak, and anger in other people because of my self-centeredness. And yes, I was on the receiving end of that when I was the one that got dumped. If this book happens to find its way into the hands of anyone that I have hurt, I am truly sorry. Really, I am. I don't have any idea on what lasting impact, if any, my actions had on others. However, I can tell you how it impacted me.

The first way that this behavior affected me is that I developed a callousness to other people's feelings. I didn't have much regard for how my actions affected them. I was more concerned about getting what I wanted.

The second thing it did was create a level of dissatisfaction in me. Sure, I was excited about a new relationship that I got, but it quickly turned to discontent. Rather than enjoy the experience of a relationship of mutual enjoyment, I would quickly turn my attention to discovering "who's next?"

As I mentioned earlier in this journal, I came to faith in God at the age of 26. I met my wife Jan when I was 29, and we got married one month short of my 32nd birthday. Where the residual effect of my youth played out was my concern about how this might be carried into marriage. While my behaviors did not continue in the same way after coming to faith as they did prior, my thoughts certainly did. I remember having a real honest conversation with God about my fear of not remaining a one-woman man after I got married. I vividly recall saying, "God, I'm kind of scared of getting married. Not that I don't want to, because I do. But I'm scared that I might not be content with just one person for the rest of my life. I've always liked girls and I really don't see how I could be satisfied with just one. However, You created marriage. It was Your idea. You are the one that said, 'A man will leave his father and mother and cleave to his wife, and the two shall become one flesh.' Even though I don't see it, I believe it because You said it. Please help to rectify this in my mind and my heart so that I will find the true contentment that you desire for a husband and wife." And has He! Oh my, how God has been faithful in this area with my wife and me. As of this writing, we have been married to each other for over 31 years and our enjoyment with each other grows greater the more time we spend together. I have never had an affair on my wife, I've never had a covetous eye for someone else, and I've never been discontent with her. She is the perfect match for me, and I am the perfect match for her (so she tells me). I cannot imagine being with anyone else.

But here is the lesson I'd like to share regarding dating. Once you have been consumed by an "addiction," you can certainly be freed of it and delivered from its grip on you. However, your mind still remembers. It remembers the places you went, the people you were with, the things you did. The "high" of your fix will sear a lasting image in your mind. These memories can creep up at any time, sometimes trying to woo you back to those self-destructive behaviors. These memories can rob you of the full amount of joy and contentment that God has intended for you. If I had to do it all over again, I would have chosen not to date at such an early age, when I had not yet learned the discipline of self-control. I would have nurtured "friend-girls" instead of girlfriends until I was ready to get serious about a lifetime mate. I have several friends that met their today spouses in high school and even junior high school. Those early relationships worked for them. I certainly did not have the maturity to nurture a romantic relationship at that age. I wish I had waited longer to start dating.

Finally, there are added risks of starting to date at a young age. After a while, the enjoyment of holding hands, hugging, and kissing is just not enough. To maintain the same thrill in the relationship, our human desire is to have more, which leads to sex. I have come to know so many people in my life whose own lives have been derailed in some way as a result of premarital sex. Emotional brokenness when the relationship ends. Unplanned pregnancy. Abortion. Sexually transmitted disease. Transmittal of HIV. Date rape. Sexual addiction. Life ambitions and career paths that have gone sideways. So much pain and so much brokenness.

My advice is to wait until you believe you are physically, mentally, emotionally, and spiritually mature to start dating and then get married. I know this may sound like a lot. However, in order to FIND the right person, you must first BE the right person. I'm certainly not alluding to perfection. Rather, to get to a point of your life where you can continue to improve your life while also making your spouse a better person. Your spouse in turn helps to make you a better person. The less baggage you bring into your marriage as a result of numerous past relationships, the better you are able to bond with the spouse that God has intended for you. That is truly what I believe is the purpose of "two becoming one flesh."

About CROP Ministries

CROP stands for Christian Rite of Passage. It is a faith-based, parent-led teen mentorship program geared for families with young teens and preteens. It's all about parents taking ownership of raising the kids that God gave them.

The development of the program came on the heels of me reading a book titled Already Gone: Why Your Kids Will Quit Church and What You Can Do to Stop It, by Ken Ham and Britt Beemer. The book studies kids raised in Christian households, reporting that three out of four will walk away from their family's faith by the time they reach their mid- to late-20's. It goes on to break down the ages at which children start to doubt their faith and what the influences are which lead to this. For many, it all starts in junior high school.

Kaylyn was 12 years old, about to turn 13, when I had finished reading this book. It occurred to me, "Who am I to expect my kid will be the one out of four that doesn't disengage from their faith, unless I do something intentional and deliberate to prepare her for the life challenges that might influence her in a negative way?" I charted out a list of topics that I felt were important to discuss with her, areas which most parents might feel unprepared or unequipped to talk about, and I wrote a lesson for each one. I then invited some of her friends, along with one of their parents, to go through each topic, so that our kids would be better equipped to face the world. Since that first group, we have mentored numerous families through this rite-of-passage.

Here is what CROP teaches. We teach that our culture does not have mile markers which help our children identify when a boy becomes a man, or a girl becomes a woman. In this absence, culture infuses its own false markers, such as the first time you smoke, take drugs, have sex, join a gang, vote, enlist in the military, etc. CROP teaches a boy becomes a man and a girl becomes a woman once their body is physically able to reproduce. When someone has the ability to procreate another human being, he or she has just been handed an adult responsibility. It doesn't mean they are mature. Maturity is a lifelong process. However, it's at this time that we as parents (and grandparents) should graduate our kids from the children's table and bring them over to the adults' table. This is the time we prepare them for what it means to be an adult: taking responsibility for your words and actions. Our job as parents is to raise our children and then release them into the world. If you have not taught them how to make good decisions, you send them out disabled and exposed to numerous paths of destruction. Our children belong to us, the parents. They do not belong to the teachers, coaches, pastors, or government. They belong to us.

However, not all parents have the tools or are capable of teaching and preparing their kids for life's challenges. How does one pass on that which they never received from their own parents? This is where CROP comes in. We are a community of parents and teens who share common beliefs, values, and commitments. We teach and mentor in group. With CROP, we strive to set up an environment where a parent only needs to do three things: show up, bring your kid, and share your own life experiences as you feel led. No homework, no preparation, no prerequisites. CROP requires a parent/grandparent/adult mentor to be present with their teens at all events. We are not a drop off/pick up program. By participating with your kid, you are involved in every lesson. CROP's job is to bring the topic to the table, and then release each parent/teen to continue the conversation afterwards.

To hear more about the story of how CROP got started, what is taught, and testimonies of others that have been mentored through the program, visit our website. If you are a family, or know of one, who is in the life stage of having an 11 – 15-year-old in the household, you might want to check it out.

www.CROPministries.org

ABOUT FAITH

Faith can be a very difficult topic for many people to talk about. Whether you call it faith, religion, spirituality or some other name, people can get put off, defensive, insecure, and even hostile when talking about spiritual matters. I have no idea what background you, our reader, is coming from. We all have an upbringing and life experiences which have greatly shaped our attitudes about the topic of faith, whether good or bad. I want to share some personal insights with you and leave it up to you to determine what you do with it. Only you are going to live your life, not me or anyone else. Only you can determine what you want to do with your future based on your past. What you do with what I'm about to share has no bearing on my life, the responsibility and outcome is solely yours.

I believe that human beings are spiritual creatures, not just physical. Yes, our human existence includes flesh and blood, physical matter that we can see and touch. The spiritual side of us is what makes humans unique from all other animals. Humans, along with animals, have a soul (which I define as the mind, will, and emotion). While we share having a body and soul with all other animals, humankind is unique in that God breathed His spirit into us, as He created us in His image. He values us over all other creatures, and we will live spiritually for all eternity.

I also believe that humankind is really good at messing up nearly everything, including religion. We have developed belief systems and then segregated people from one another based on these man-made religious orders. Choose one, and then challenge all the others into believing yours is correct and everyone else is wrong. We allow very little room for honest discussion and reasoning with one another and tend to be quick to shut out others who don't believe as we do. As a result, there are numerous man-made religious systems in the world today. Do a quick online search and you will be led to sites that estimate that there are over 4,000 religious belief systems in the world. So go ahead, choose one! And saying you don't choose a particular one is in itself a choice. Call it the religion of secularism.

Simply put, I believe there is one God who created all things. All that is seen and unseen, discovered and yet to be discovered. This one God created it all and holds everything together. He created humans because He loves us, not because He needed us. He is perfect love and lacks nothing. As a parent, I think we know that when we have children of our own that they will bring us great joy and love but will bring us pain and disappointment as well. We have some sort of knowledge of the sacrifices we will have to make over our lifetime for our children, and we recognize that they will disobey us over and over again despite knowing things from our own understanding and experience that they may not yet know from their own. Yet, despite the expense, sacrifice and pain to raise a child, the love we have for them and from them outweighs the cost. It's worth the risk.

So we have kids. Our kids have their own will, and they will choose whether or not to follow our guidance, oftentimes despite us knowing what's best for them. Children begin to exercise their free will from the time they are infants, and it gets stronger as they grow older. Their life choices can either bring us great joy or great pain, but ultimately, they are solely responsible for the choices they make.

So it is with God, the spiritual Father. If you are one of many, many people who recoil at the mention of the name "father" because of trauma inflicted by your own broken, earthly father, understand that the creator God is THE perfect Father who loves you more than you can ever know. There is nothing you can do to cause Him to love you more or love you less. His love for you is perfect. Just like a good parent, it pains Him to see when we ourselves are hurt, whether at our own hands or the hands of others. Can perfect God have stopped and intervened in the midst of some trauma that was being done to you? Sure, I think so. But if He does, then where does He draw the line? Think of all the things you have done in your life which hurt other people. Wouldn't He have to shove His foot in the door of your life for every misstep you made, in order for Him to be fair? I've certainly done my share of harm towards other people in the wake of my own selfish acts. If God threw the penalty flag on every instance, both great and small, would we really live a life of liberty? One of free will? Or would we simply become obedient robot soldiers who are forced to do what God wills, when He wills, how He wills. That is what I would call forced love. I believe free love is when we are the object of receiving love and we have the choice of responding in kind to that love.

It's that very thing, the choice to disobey God's will for our life, which separates us spiritually from Him. He is perfect, He is pure, He has no fault in Him. We, which includes you and me, have made choices in our life in disobedience to God, just as a child disobeys a parent. Disobedience always results in consequence. When a child disobeys a parent, they are subject to discipline. When a civilian disobeys the law, they are subject to fine and/or imprisonment. When a human disobeys God, we are subject to separation from Him. In His perfection He cannot have fellowship with our imperfection.

This part requires practically no convincing. Whatever belief system, if any, has been sown into your childhood, I believe we have inherent knowledge of when we are disobedient to what God would desire of us. The more disobedience we practice, the more we separate ourselves from Him. I've never known a person who has lived in outright rebellion and drew nearer to the real God in the process. People can deceive themselves sometimes into thinking their harmful self-serving acts on other people are being done "in the name of god or religion", but in reality, they are delusional. God never desires we do unjust intentional harm to someone, whether friend or enemy. When one feels that God is distant, it's not because He moved.

What, then, is God's perfect solution to humankind's imperfection problem? It's simple. Jesus. Jesus is both fully God and fully man. I know, this can be hard to get your head around sometimes. God sent Jesus to us, to you, to fill in the gap between you and Him.

Look at it this way. If you had a message to communicate to an entire colony of ants, and you had unlimited power in your ability to communicate with them, how would you do it? Would you yell and shout at them? Would you print and hold up signs? Would you send in an anteater to keep them in line and destroy the ones that got out of line? Or would you, too, become an ant? An ant that looks, thinks, shares mannerisms with the other ants but is set apart as unique and special in order to lead the ants into a better way.

So it is with God. He became one of us, the person of Jesus, to lead us into a better way. To stand in defense of us who are willing to allow Him to do so. What do I mean by that?

Imagine you committed a crime. This crime was a very severe crime. One in which there is no doubt that you are guilty, and the punishment for your crime is the death penalty. There is no other penalty that is available to you, and the crime warrants the punishment. As you are on your final death row march to your fair and just destiny, you meet someone who loves you very much, who does not want to see you perish. While that person committed no crime, he offers to trade his life for yours so that you can be set free. The judge has one guilty party (you) and he needs to impose capital judgement on one person (you or the friend). The judge cannot impose the penalty on both. Only on one. What do you do? Do you take the punishment, or do you allow someone to take it for you?

Perhaps you acknowledge that you are the guilty one, and you refuse to receive this free gift that was just offered to you: someone taking your guilt upon themselves so that you are released from it and are set free. Free to start over. Free to choose a new life. Free to feel that burden of guilt and shame lifted from you so that you can be the person that you were created to be.

That is what Jesus has done for you. As both God and as man, He has chosen to substitute His life for yours so that you can be set free. You can start new again. You can be spiritually reborn in order to be reunited with the very One who created you because He loves you.

Here is the part that is so hard yet is so easy. You have to choose. Only you can choose for yourself. No one can choose for you. Do you remain spiritually separated from God, which He doesn't desire but loves you enough to let you choose if you want to reciprocate your love for Him? Or do you accept His perfect love gift to you, Jesus, who has no guilt in Him but accepts your guilt upon Himself so that you are forgiven?

This is what makes this issue of religion and belief systems so easy. There really are not over 4,000 religious belief systems in the world that humankind has created. There are only 2, the ones that God provides. That is, you either believe Jesus is who HE said He is, or you don't. Forget the confusion, forget the labels, forget the historical aspects of world religions. Do you believe Jesus is who HE said He is, or don't you? When compared to all other spiritual leaders throughout human history, He has no equal.

If you are looking for truth, then understand this: truth is not someTHING, it is someONE. Jesus is the one who said, "I am the way, I am the TRUTH, I am the life. Nobody comes to the Father but through Me." Jesus never said, "Go to church". He said, "Come to Me". Does that sound too narrow? Perhaps. But think about this. Most large chasms are crossed via a narrow bridge. Stray from the straight path and you are doomed to destruction. Keep your eyes straight ahead, on the path before you, and you are bound towards safety.

God created us to have relationship with Him. He desires that we remain connected spiritually. God is spirit. How does spirit communicate? With spirit. That is, the spirit He breathed into us at the creation of humans. When we wander away from that spiritual aspect of us, then we tend to fill that void with something else. Alcohol, drugs, sexuality, anger, fear, hopelessness and other self-destructive behaviors. God wants to release you from the bond that those things hold on you by having you accept the perfect gift of Jesus that He offers you. He never intended you to carry the heavy burdens of guilt, regret and shame that life heaps upon us. He wants to take that burden away. So how do you do that?

Again, very simple. Believe what I just outlined. Admit that you have been disobedient to God. Ask for forgiveness. Acknowledge that Jesus is the only way to be forgiven and ask God to help you to turn your life around. Ask Him to free you of the burdens you are carrying. He will. I promise.

The beginning of this new life simply starts by saying out loud something like this:

"God, I now see what you already know. I have been disobedient to you. I have lived my life for me, and not for you. You desire I live an abundant life, but my decisions have kept me from that. I confess that I am a sinner, and I want to be forgiven. I believe that you sent your son, Jesus, to set me free from my sin and my behaviors. Jesus, I ask that you come into my life. I surrender my spirit to yours, so that you can mold me and shape me into the person you have intended me to be. Thank you for loving me. I pray this in the name of Jesus, amen".

That's it. Pretty simple. God loves you too much to make it difficult. It's not the words you say that are magical, it's the attitude of your heart. If your heart was genuine when you prayed this prayer out loud, God will run to you. As the perfect Father, He wants you to come home, and to enjoy all that He has intended for you. His ways will always be the best ways. It's now up to you to learn what they are.

Next steps? Well, there are several. But don't be too concerned about looking too far down that road. God will show you the way. Just take each step one at a time. Here is what I would suggest.

Tell someone what you just did. Don't tell just anyone, because not everyone will understand. Rather, tell someone who you know is a believer in Jesus. Chances are, you have someone in your life that you know has exhibited the kind of godly behavior that reflects the way of Jesus. Tell this person you prayed to God for forgiveness and that you invited Jesus into your life. As a newborn (spiritual) baby, this person will most likely celebrate your new "birth" with you and mentor you into your spiritual growth.

Purchase a bible and download a bible app or two. Once you start reading, you will start growing. Remember, you knew much more in sixth grade than you ever knew in first grade. The more you read the bible, the more you will grow in your understanding of spiritual things. Each bible will have some sort of reading plan that you can follow, or you can simply start reading the book of John to understand the life and work of Jesus.

Get connected with a local bible teaching church. Remember, there are several "denominations" of churches, part of the 4,000+ that we talked about earlier. It's really critical that you find a church that believes 100% that Jesus is who He said He is, and that the church doesn't water down the message. Hopefully the person that you told in step #1 can lead you to a good church.

Start listening to radio programs, podcasts, and music which are about Jesus. You will be amazed at how this will begin to nourish your spirit and soul.

Ask lots of questions of people who are more spiritually mature and knowledgeable. Just because you don't know about something doesn't mean that there isn't a great explanation. Every good question has a great answer. You just have to be willing to ask. I've been a follower of Jesus for over 37 years and there are things I still don't know. That's ok. That's part of the thrill of the journey. A website and app that I really like is www.GotQuestions.org .

Be aware of this fact: just as there is the spiritual reality of a God who wants to bring you home and be reconciled with Him, there is another competing spiritual reality, your own sin nature and Satan, who want to keep you separated from God and lead you down a path of destruction. This battle is real. It's like two wolves fighting with one another for dominance. One wolf is for good. It is peace, love, hope, humility, compassion, and faith. The other wolf is for evil. It is anger, bitterness, jealousy, indulgence and self-destruction. This battle will rage on within you for as long as you have breath in your lungs. So which wolf do you think will win this battle? The one you feed. Whenever you make mistakes and realize you have been disobedient to God, do not be discouraged. Simply admit to Him that you made a mistake, confess it to God, ask for forgiveness and He will forgive you. Your spiritual connection will be restored. Remember, the larger the "good wolf" grows within you, the smaller the "bad wolf" will become in your life. God's Spirit will give you the strength you need for the battle.

One final word of encouragement: if you prayed this prayer and it truly reflects the attitude of your heart, do you want to know something really cool? The bible says that all the angels in heaven are rejoicing! Imagine that: ALL the angels are rejoicing and celebrating, for you! What could be better than that?

To Those Who Choose Not to Accept This Message

I still love you. God still loves you. Nothing will change that. However, He and I respect your choice. We respect your wishes. We love you too much to force anything on you. As I said previously, forced love is not real love. I have had numerous conversations with people who have rejected the concept of God, even been hostile towards it. In my conversations with them, I have come to learn this. Every one of them shares one thing in common, and it's the same thing: they experienced a deep wound, a deep pain in their life. "If God is loving," they reason, "and if He is capable of doing anything, why didn't He save me from this wound? But because He didn't, then either He's not loving, or else He doesn't exist. So don't talk to me about some loving 'god.'"

If this is you, then let me say how very sorry I am. I'm sorry that we do live in a broken world filled with hurt and damaged people who inflict pain on others because of their own failures and selfish indulgences. This wound was not your fault, and the current state of the world is certainly not as God intended. He gave us the freedom to make our own decisions, and oftentimes these decisions hurt others.

Yet, God does not want you to live with this pain. He does not want you to carry this heavy burden. He, too, knows someone who has been deeply hurt, deeply wounded. It's His son, Jesus. Jesus knows your burden, too, because He carries all our burdens upon Himself. He tells us to cast our troubles upon Him because his yoke is easy, and His burden is light. This is true, whether or not you believe it. So what have you got to lose? You can continue to walk through life carrying this unbearable load on your own, or you can change course and let Him who is able relieve you from this pain. I have seen so many people in my life who were in this situation, and God has completely transformed their life for the better.

Keep this in mind, and I say this with all love and compassion. Those who choose to reject God and remain separated from Him will one day get their wish. This may sound harsh and unreasonable but consider this. Would a truly just and loving God force someone to live spiritually united with Him for all eternity if that person rejected Him his or her entire life? God's answer will always be, "As you wish". Do you want to be restored to God by admitting that you have disobeyed Him, and asking for forgiveness? As you wish. Do you want nothing to do with God, because you believe the path you are on is better than what He offers you? As you wish.

If all of this still does not resonate with you, I truly hope that one day it will. I vividly recall every person who tried to share this message with me in my early adult years and I was not ready to receive it. Thankfully, I came to the awareness of this truth at the age of 26 and my life has never been the same since then. I would not trade anything in the world for my relationship with God through Jesus.

ABOUT THE AUTHORS

Kaylyn Martinez

Kaylyn is the inspiration for the CROP Ministries program and is officially the first graduate of the first class ever conducted by her dad. She shares to this day the impact that the program had on her relationship with her dad and with God. Kaylyn has two beautiful little boys named Anthony and Cayden. She is currently homeschooling her oldest son, Anthony. She loves to cook and bake. She can't wait for the day her sons go through the CROP program.

Mark Martinez

Mark was born and raised in the Los Angeles area. He went to Arcadia High School in Arcadia and San Diego State University, where he earned his B.S. degree in Business Administration. Mark has had careers in both business and in Christian ministry, and he is the founder and creator of CROP Ministries. He was inspired to write and develop the program for his oldest daughter, Kaylyn, when she was 12 years old. He recognizes the importance of a rite-of-passage for young teens and was unable to find a comprehensive parent-led teen mentorship program, so he wrote one. He and his wife, Jan, have been married for over 31 years and have their two daughters, Kaylyn and Elizabeth.

www.ingramcontent.com/pod-product-compliance
Lightning Source LLC
Chambersburg PA
CBHW020927090426
42736CB00010B/1069